William Allison was born in Perthshire and began his career in journalism as a reporter with D.C. Thomson Publications in Scotland. He held various posts on the *Daily Express*, including those of associate news editor and features editor, and was assistant editor of the *London Evening News*. He lives in London with his wife Shirley and two student sons and is chief executive of Syndicated Features, London's international newspaper and magazine agency.

John Fairley comes from Liverpool. He worked on the *Evening Post* in Bristol and the *Evening Standard* in London before moving to the B.B.C. and then Yorkshire Television. He and actress Jill Barron have two young daughters. They divide their time between London and a cottage in Yorkshire.

THE MONOCLED MUTINEER

William Allison and John Fairley

QUARTET BOOKS LONDON MELBOURNE NEW YORK

First published by Quartet Books Limited 1978
A member of the Namara Group
27 Goodge Street, London W1P 1FD

Copyright © 1978 by William Allison and John Fairley

Lines from 'Goodbye-ee' © 1918 reproduced by permission
of Francis Day & Hunter Ltd.

ISBN 0 70432154 8

Photosetting by Red Lion Setters, Holborn, London

Printed and bound in Great Britain by
The Garden City Press Limited
Letchworth, Hertfordshire SG6 1JS

Dedicated to the men who successfully defied the worst brutalities of an old style militarism, which, if it had been allowed to persist, could well have meant Britain and her Allies losing the First World War, thereby drastically altering the course of world history.

To Frank Durham and John Radgick for great forbearance extended over a long period of time.

And in loving memory of Paul Giorgi.

List of Illustrations

Acknowledgements

Our greatest thanks must go to the many veterans of the Étaples base camp from all over Britain and the Commonwealth who wrote and spoke to us about their memories of the Bull Ring and the Mutiny. Many are quoted by name in the text. We have also had great help from the residents of Étaples, particularly M. Achille Caron, photographer and historian of the town.

Friends and relatives of Percy Toplis assisted us, as did Arthur Rayment, who encountered Toplis in his post-war career, and Mr William Stephens, who had memories of his wartime activities. The published personal reminiscences of Edwin Woodhall (*Detective and Secret Service Days*, Jarrolds, London) and Lady Angela Forbes (*Memories and Base Details*, Hutchinson and Co., London) have been invaluable to us, as have the journalists' accounts in *John Bull*, *World's Pictorial News*, the *New York Tribune*, the *Andover Advertiser*, the *Yorkshire Post* and the Penrith *Observer*.

We have also had great help from the staff of the Imperial War Museum, the Public Records Office and the British Newspaper Library, and we have drawn considerable background material from the extensive literature about the First World War.

The Wilfred Owen quotation on page 72 is taken from *Wilfred Owen: Collected Letters*, edited by H. Owen and J. Bell (London, 1967).

Throughout we have had enormous help and support from Murray Allison and Jill Barron in the exhaustive research involved, and from photographers Tony Timmington and Richard Cackett.

Prologue

Percy Toplis was, and remains, the spark of this story. A pit-boy who tricked his way confidently through London high society, a womanizer, an outlaw, he was to be hunted by the Secret Service, to break his way out of prison under threat of a death sentence, and finally to be shot down by the police in what was as spectacular and preposterous an ambush as the constabulary have ever mounted in England.

But the pursuit of the story of Toplis was to lead us into history, into one of the central enigmas of the First World War: the manner in which millions of men apparently went obediently and meekly to the slaughter at the behest of the politicians and the generals. The French Army did rebel, and almost cast away the war. But hitherto the image of the British Army has been one of unquestioning obedience and unbending discipline. Our search for Toplis was to lead us through a succession of outrageous adventures into the centre of a huge mutiny of the British Army previously recorded only as tiny glimpses in memoirs of more glorious moments.

Even the most sceptical authors writing about the First World War make no mention of the six days during which a sizeable section of the British Army rebelled and threatened Field-Marshal Haig's autumn offensive against Passchendaele in 1917. One author, R. H. Mottram, in 1929 condemned this omission as a disgraceful conspiracy to conceal an event which should not have been hushed up. He excused his own failure to write on the subject by confessing that he did not know the truth about the mutiny, adding that perhaps no one knew the truth. But sixty years later there are still, the length and breadth of Britain, ordinary men who remember with both pride and bitterness the time when thousands of Scots, Australian, New Zealand and English soldiers defied the Army High Command in the rebellion of Étaples — and won. If Toplis is occasionally submerged in the swell of this secret history, which the military authorities are still at pains to suppress, then that is no more than he might have wished, or expected.

1

Percy Toplis was ambushed by three policemen near a country church on a hot summer's evening in
June 1920. Worshippers coming out from evensong scattered
for cover among the gravestones to avoid being caught up in
the exchange of gunfire. The local chief constable's son,
armed with an automatic pistol, roared up to join in.
Toplis's killing, at the age of 23, was brutal, and its manner
unprecedented, but it also came as a great relief to the
highest authorities in the War Office and the Secret Service.
For with him were buried, for sixty years at least, some of
the darker secrets of the First World War.

At the time the case aroused a small amount of adverse
comment in the *Manchester Guardian*, slight praise in the
Yorkshire Post, total approval in local newspapers, and
some muted protest at Westminster. It took a jury just three
minutes to record a verdict of justifiable homicide. The
chief constable who, it was claimed, had authorized the
operation was awarded the CBE and then, within weeks,
mysteriously resigned. Even in death, Percy Toplis continued
to blight the lives of the establishment.

Toplis had been handsome, debonair, a natural actor, a
fair pianist, a renowned philanderer. He had a wild sense of

humour. Even when on the run for his life, he ostentatiously affected a gold-rimmed monocle. But, unknown to the newspaper readers who devoured the scandalous details of his post-war career, he was also the most extravagant anti-hero of the First World War. At a time when he ought to have been dead, executed by firing squad in accordance with rough-and-ready wartime justice, he was rejoining the British Forces with arrogant ease, confident he would not be touched.

It was a very grateful authority that made quiet heroes of the men who finally gunned him down, and who then swiftly swept him under the sod into a pauper's grave overlooking the hills and lakes of Ullswater. The cemetery register simply states: 'Shot dead by police at Plumpton.'

But there are those alive today who still remember Percy Toplis with affection, respect and admiration. They include his closest childhood friend, Ernest Leah of Bilsthorpe, Mansfield. Leah looked so like his friend that he was once actually arrested by police in a case of mistaken identity when the countrywide manhunt was on for Toplis. As Leah recalls:

'He was my best friend. A lovely lad. Today he would have been regarded as one of those intellectual socialists. Then, he had no chance at all. Mind you, he was a bit of a tearaway, was Percy.'

Ernest Leah's brother Raymond, a local councillor in Alfreton, Derbyshire, still keeps Toplis's army belt as a treasured memento.

This, then, is the story of the monocled tearaway, Private alias Lieutenant/Captain/Colonel Percy Toplis, who made the biggest single-handed contribution to the almost unknown mutiny of the British Army in France in the First World War.

In June 1920, less than three years after that rebellion, the authorities no doubt excused themselves for the manner of his death with the thought that Toplis had been too dangerous to bring to trial. The country was not yet ready for regrets and recriminations. Or for a first-hand, eye-witness account of a mutiny which had officially never happened.

14

Even today, the Ministry of Defence shies away from the word 'mutiny'. It prefers the word 'disturbances', which was the description used in a secret army record of the time. But mutiny it was, and it lasted six desperate days, involved thousands of troops and finished with the authorities surrendering and a brigadier-general being relieved of his command. Toplis's control of another British army — an army of deserters behind the front line — was so complete that when the mutiny brought about a clean sweep of military police personnel, the first and most important task of the new commander, a secret service agent, Edwin Woodhall, was to track Toplis down. But Toplis, as he was to do so many times again, turned Houdini and escaped to thumb his nose at the military and the police through another three years of immaculate effrontery.

But then he had been doing that to authorities of every kind since he was 11 years old.

2

Toplis made the last entry in his diary on Saturday, 5 June 1920, and it read, 'Some search, Carlisle' — not a phrase intended to be in praise of his pursuers, but more of a contemptuous dismissal of their puerile efforts. Since he made that entry while relaxing in the depot of the Border Regiment at Carlisle — where, despite being the most wanted man and the most notorious soldier in England, he had been fed and lodged without question — he was perhaps entitled to be scathing. From the first days of his desertion from the army in wartime France, Percy Toplis had lived dangerously.

This was particularly the case when he was short of money, a state from which he occasionally suffered, and one that was with him once again that fatal weekend. In such circumstances, Toplis had always sought and been given succour in the lion's den; he knew that was where searchers were least likely to look.

On the penultimate day of his life he stuck to his common practice, and seemingly went unrecognized as he mingled in the Carlisle depot with scores of regular army troops. Or it may have been that, whether for reasons of fear or sympathy, no one was prepared to turn him in. Next

16

morning he slung his kitbag over his shoulder, and in the khaki uniform of an army corporal, still complete with puttees, went marching down the Scotland Road towards Penrith. It was a warm day, and Mrs Mary Taylor (84), daughter of a gamekeeper at Newbigging, remembers him calling in for, and being given, a refreshing cup of tea.

Toplis then resumed his tramp over the hill from Newbigging and down into the valley towards the villages of Low and High Hesket. Midway between those two hamlets, a small Wesleyan Chapel (1869) had then, as it has still, a soft, inviting stretch of well-kept lawn by the roadside. Toplis sat down there, and was so engrossed in a Sunday newspaper account of his shoot-up of a policeman and gamekeeper in the Scottish Highlands a few days before that he failed to spot the approach of Police Constable Alfred Fulton, village constable for both Low and High Hesket.

Fulton, a military type of figure with a wide, waxed moustache, had been in the police for thirteen years. Until then his most dangerous adversaries had been the local poachers. Toplis did not wait for the questioning to begin. He quickly closed his newspaper, looked up at Fulton and said, 'Let's cut it short. I am, I suppose, what you would call a deserter, but really I am only absent without leave. I have been away from my depot since June the second, but I am on my way back now.'

Fulton asked him for some identification, and Toplis produced a driver's licence which carried the name, 'John Henry Thompson'. Fulton accepted Toplis's offer of the newspaper and watched him tramp on further south. As he told the coroner later, 'I then let him go on the expectation he was going to his depot.'

At this point Mrs Fulton proved to be brighter than her husband. When Fulton got to his home, a quarter of a mile away, she greeted him with: 'Alf, about half an hour ago I saw a soldier pass the window, and he looked to me as if he could be that Toplis man everybody's been looking for.' Fulton sat down, searched through his file of 'wanted' descriptions and decided his wife might just be right. Out

17

came his pedal-cycle, on went the bicycle clips and off he sped down the Scotland Road in pursuit. This time the constable got the confirmation he was seeking without the need for questioning.

The bells of St Mary's Church, High Hesket, were ringing for evensong when Toplis, with gun drawn, watched from behind a clump of trees near the churchyard as Fulton probed his way through plantation undergrowth, the first available cover, parting the bushes with his truncheon and calling out every so often, 'Coo-ee, are you there? Where are you?'

Toplis went on watching for a little time, then ended the hide-and-seek game suddenly. He stepped from behind the trees, levelled his Webley 6 at Fulton's head and said, without hesitation, 'If it's Toplis you're after, I'm your man.'

Fulton was later to tell journalists that he felt the church bells were tolling a personal dirge for him. He gazed fixedly down the barrel of the gun, a mere four yards away, and only partly stopped trembling when Toplis, in surprisingly kindly, avuncular tones, addressed him further: 'I was forced to shoot that lot at Tomintoul, and if you go on being a bad lad I may have to shoot you too. Now why don't you just throw down your handcuffs and truncheon and beat it?'

The shocked but grateful policeman did exactly as ordered, and as Toplis backed into the undergrowth, still with gun pointing, Fulton just as slowly backed into the open fields which separated him from home. With his free left hand Toplis gave him a friendly, farewell wave and called out, 'You must be the smartest lawman in England', before disappearing back into the trees. Fulton, still shaking and gasping, quickly turned and ran home across the fields. His life had been spared, but any gratitude he felt was not going to be shared by his superiors.

The men who had hunted Toplis in the past curiously seem to have taken to emulating his own love of disguise. On that Sunday night, the act of the quick-change became positively infectious. Back home, Fulton hurriedly slipped out of uniform and into goggles, cap, tweed jacket and knickerbockers, and on his high-handlebar motor-cycle roared into Penrith police headquarters eight miles away where he gasped out the news that the infamous outlaw Toplis was heading into town. Fulton had good reason to be certain, for he had seen Toplis for the third time, still on the road to Penrith. Although by now heavily disguised, Fulton had increased his speed and given him a wide berth.

While Fulton was breaking the news at Penrith, the teenage Misses Richardson of Low Plains Farm giggled and nudged each other as they watched a young man shaving and washing himself at an animal drinking trough in woodland known as Thiefside, on the edge of the Penrith road. When he started to change out of army uniform into civilian clothing, they ran off shrieking.

Pandemonium and panic are the only possible words to describe what happened next at Penrith and elsewhere. The two men in receipt of Fulton's information, Sergeant Robert Bertram and Inspector William Ritchie, were noted more for their splendid physique than their erudition. Big, bluff Bertram had been a boy sailor in the Royal Navy before joining the police, where he excelled in teaching recruits jiu-jitsu and boxing. Just as big and hearty was Inspector Ritchie, a Cumberland wrestler of great renown who had lately won the all-weights championship at Grasmere.

The two men decided that the fact that Toplis was on his way was not knowledge with which they should be exclusively burdened. They passed it on to Superintendent Tom Oldcorn at his home, and he rushed to the police station to telephone Deputy Chief Constable Joseph Barron. Barron phoned the news to Chief Constable Norman de Courcy Parry at home, and he in turn consulted Scotland Yard, which then irritated Home Office officials by calling them away from dinner for telephone discussions. The question of dealing with Percy Toplis had to go to the highest level. And Toplis would have been supremely gratified by the enormous uproar his appearance in Cumberland was creating throughout both the county and the country. Penrith police

19

secured all the trunk telephone wires for the purposes of
their consultations, which ranged from army headquarters
at Bulford, Wiltshire, across to London and up to Scotland.

An hour after Fulton first broke the news, Toplis was still
plodding on towards Penrith, and the police force was still
sorting itself out. Eventually, at around seven o'clock, a
decision emerged. Someone in that long chain from
Cumberland to Whitehall decided that a military-style
operation had to be mounted. Every off-duty policeman,
and the entire special constabulary, numbering fifty men,
were called out, forming a cordon round the whole area,
stretching from Caldbeck and Fenruddock in the west to the
foot of the Pennines in the east, while every road and lane to
the north and south of Penrith had a police post. Nearly 160
Cumberland policemen were on the Toplis trail.

Guns were handed out to those who were manning check-
points considered vital. The guns that were to matter were
handed to Inspector Ritchie and Sergeant Bertram by
Superintendent Oldcorn. Meanwhile, the chief constable's
22-year-old son, Norman de Courcy Parry, Jnr, was turning
out with his own small Belgian automatic, one of several
'unofficial' souvenirs he had brought home from the war.

When the chief constable first received the Toplis alert at
the family home, Barton House, on the edge of Penrith, the
call had been taken by young Parry, a self-admitted
wayward son. He had stayed close to the telephone so as to
overhear some of his father's consultations and discussions.
This young ex-officer of the Seaforth Highlanders was just
emerging from a bad spell of health during which he had
suffered severe headaches caused by a head-wound received
in France, a wound which had caused him many sleepless
nights long afterwards. But he was slowly recovering; he was
anxious to assist and eager for adventure. The father was
just as anxious not to thwart his son, and at the same time
was grateful for any offer of help in the crisis. He sent him to
man a road-block at Alston, a spot far removed from the
potential danger zone on the Penrith-Carlisle road. But
young Parry disobeyed, having overheard where it was

hoped to spring the main trap. He hid his gun inside his jacket.

Back at Penrith police station, the craze for change was once again in full swing. Ritchie and Bertram were out of their uniforms and struggling into any ill-fitting civilian clothes they could find, which they topped off with caps, mufflers and raincoats, ignoring the heat of the night. Fulton also put on a raincoat, despite the fact that he was already in civilian clothes. To round off their impersonation of Sunday trippers, they then commandeered a blue, open four-seater Armstrong car from the Crown Hotel and appointed one of the part-time barmen, Edward Spruce, as driver.

On his ten horsepower 1,000-cc American motor-cycle, a machine capable of attaining the then phenomenal speed of 80 m.p.h., Parry Jnr raced through Penrith's main street to get into the act. Strollers in the late sunshine scattered like hens as he roared along to catch up with the Armstrong as it turned out of Hunter's Lane, site of the police head-quarters. Young Parry then talked the gullible Ritchie into believing that the chief constable specifically wanted him to be with the 'armoured brigade'. And so this strangest of all police convoys, led by a goggled, leather-helmeted civilian motor-cyclist, moved north on to the Carlisle highway, the car driven by barman Spruce doing a steady 45 m.p.h., with Fulton in the front passenger seat and the gun-carrying Ritchie and Bertram standing on either running-board, clinging to the sides, capped, mufflered and raincoated.

Just north of the crossroads village of Plumpton, four miles from Penrith, the motley crew of apparent joy-riders passed a neat, well-shaven trilby-hatted, brown-suited young man carrying a brown-paper parcel. They were nearly a mile past their target before the fact dawned on Fulton. He shouted up to Ritchie, who was grimly holding on to the inside of Fulton's front passenger seat, 'Sorry, sir, but it has just struck me. That man we passed could have been Toplis. He must have cleaned himself up and changed his clothes since I last saw him.'

21

Ritchie roared across Fulton at Spruce, 'Turn round!'

In their tension and excitement the car had also over-taken its leader, young Parry, who had not allowed the thrill of the chase to overcome his powers of observation or sense of suspicion. Just before he drew level with the pedestrian coming towards him on the east side of the road, Parry had stopped his motor-cycle on the west side, pretending it had broken down. With his cycle between him and Toplis on the other side of the road, he peered through the machine's framework and identified the face under the hat as that of Toplis, who was now standing stock-still, taking note of the strange antics that were going on in his honour.

When Parry saw the car had turned round and was coming back towards him, he gave the thumbs-up sign to Ritchie, indicating that the figure on the other side of the road was their man.

Ritchie shouted to his driver, 'Now slower this time, Ted, and nearer to him.'

Instead, the car gathered speed and veered away from Toplis and past him for the second time.

Ritchie shouted at Spruce, 'For Christ's sake, Ted! What the hell's the matter with you?'

But the barman was too terrified to hear him, and with cloth cap pulled well down over a chalk-white face, he took a firmer grip on the steering-wheel, crouched low over it and started heading back towards Penrith at a maximum 50 m.p.h. Ritchie had an answer to his question in the look of absolute terror on Spruce's face. The car started to rock dangerously, threatening to dislodge the cumbersome Cumberland wrestler and the burly boxer from the running-boards.

Fulton had now joined his superiors in their efforts to get Spruce to stop. He pummelled the driver in the side as all three kept shouting, 'Stop! For God's sake, stop!' But Spruce had put nearly a mile of roadway and a bend between him and the outlaw before he could be persuaded to pull up out of sight of both Toplis and Parry. The hunt seemed to be turning into a black comedy with more than a touch of the

22

Keystone Kops, then at the height of their movie fame. Inspector Ritchie was beginning to suspect that perhaps Spruce had been drinking rather than serving back at the Crown.

Angrily, Ritchie yelled at Spruce, 'This is where we get off, and you get to hell out of the way.'

Spruce gratefully and hastily revved up his engine and vanished from the story in a splutter of gravel and stones.

The strain and the heat were beginning to tell on all three officers. Fulton's waxed moustache was starting to disintegrate at each end. Even the two well-trained athletes were sweating profusely. Grimly, Ritchie instructed his fellow officers, 'We can't go on like this. This is where we have to get down to business.' With his drawn gun he waved them to the western side of the road. There he motioned them to take up a position in a line directly behind him, concealed from view by the high wall of the Romanway Farm rose garden. Immediately behind Ritchie was Bertram with his gun, and behind him was Fulton.

Although Toplis had temporarily succeeded in fooling the police by his new appearance, their 'disguise' had raised his suspicions, and when the car had passed him and Parry the second time, he crossed the road to where Parry continued to crouch beside his cycle, tinkering with the engine. Parry had the small Belgian automatic pistol hidden inside his coat. For a moment he thought of trying to use it. Then Toplis half-drew his Webley from his inside jacket pocket. It was too late, much too late. By the time Parry could have extracted the gun and cocked it he would have been dead. Toplis said, 'Who are these men who keep passing us in that car?'

It was Parry's turn to start sweating. He pretended he had not seen the gun and evenly replied, 'I think they're just out for a joy-ride.'

Toplis snapped back, 'Then why did you give them the thumbs-up sign?'

23

Parry again got his nerves under control and reassured him, 'Well, I know two of them and I was just trying to signal them to get me some assistance because my bike has broken down.'

Toplis let his gun slide back into his pocket. Absurdly, it crossed Parry's mind to start the bike and offer Toplis a lift on the pillion. He thought better of it, and Toplis turned away and resumed his walk south towards Romanway Farm. Parry abandoned the cycle and followed him about twenty-five yards behind. Once again he thought about firing. But he remembered that it took a very good marksman to hit a moving target with a revolver at that range.

Toplis turned round sharply: 'When I told you not to follow me I meant just that.'

Parry shouted back, 'Don't worry. I've told you. All I want is some assistance with my bike.'

Stragglers from evensong at the Church of St John the Evangelist were still grouped around the door in conversation when the ambush opened up. The two civilian-clad figures, Ritchie and Bertram, rushed out, guns blazing, followed by Fulton. The church worshippers flung themselves flat among the gravestones. Toplis broke into a run in the direction in which he had been walking, towards Penrith, turning to shoot it out as he fled. Ritchie is alleged to have shouted, 'Stop! Pull up,' but no one else spoke. The only exchange was one of gunfire.

Toplis kept running a few yards at a time, then turning to shoot from a crouched position, his feet planted firmly and widely apart in an effort to steady his aim. Young Parry, closing in behind the lawmen, continued to be riveted by the wild, staring eyes of the outlaw and the sneering contempt on his face.

Both Bertram and Ritchie kept firing as they chased him on to a grassy slope at the side of the road. Ritchie was only four feet away from Toplis when he started to topple slowly forwards down the slight slope towards him. The outlaw's left hand suddenly clutched the left side of his chest, his right hand drooped, still shooting defiantly, but wildly and aimlessly now, into the ground by his own feet.

Still in slow motion, he rose to his toes in a hopeless, last effort to rally before finally crashing forwards and downwards into Ritchie's arms. The only sound he made throughout was a deep sigh before his head slumped on to his injured chest. The trilby fell from his head, upturned to become wedged between his own body and that of Ritchie and provided a receptacle for the blood gushing from the fatal wound.

They stretched him out in the sunset on the south side of the road in the middle of which lay the brown-paper parcel containing his selection of army and RAF clothing. He had dropped it there when the shooting started. The string had broken, and the contents were spilled on to the road. His precious, gold-rimmed monocle remained in his pocket. On the north side of the road the church organist continued to play the congregation out. The worshippers had thrown themselves down when they heard the noise of the gun battle — a noise which the organist failed to hear above the sound of his own music. He continued to play. Down the aisle and through the open church door the deep strains floated on the stillness of the night summer air ... The day Thou gavest, Lord, is ended. Darkness falls at Thy behest. It was a most satisfactory conclusion for the gentlemen in Whitehall. The man at the centre of the most unpalatable secret of the First World War had been silenced. A career which had irritated and confounded the police, the army and the government for a dozen years was ended.

25

3

The Larceny Act (1861) is imprecise about the manner in which birching shall be carried out. The victim, or at least his buttocks, are expected to be naked. But the method of holding him down is left to local initiative. He can be forced to bend down with his head locked between the knees of a seated police officer. Or he can be held down over a bench or table. Or, in areas where the frequency of the punishment justified it, there might be a specially constructed tripod or triangle with straps for the hands above the head and straps for the feet at the base. This device, though an expense, had the advantage of keeping the victim rigid.

Percy Toplis was just past his eleventh birthday when he first met the Mansfield method. This was an ingenious fusion of cheapness and efficiency. An ordinary table had been fitted with four iron clamps: two on the legs and two at the top corners. Leather straps ran through the stanchions. Toplis was a skinny boy, and the straps had to have an extra hole punched to secure his ankles. From this point on the procedure was as everywhere else. In the corner of the bare whitewashed room, standing in a bucket, was a bundle of birch twigs, with the top two feet bound by wire to form a handle. The rest looked like the sweeping end of a garden broom.

'Are you ready?' Then, in the absence of a response: 'Lay on!'

The first stroke, across the buttocks 'with sufficient force', was not expected to break the skin. The second, third and fourth, 'at proper intervals' to avoid any impression of anger, fell in the same locality. It was important to keep away from the area of the kidneys, though no protective belt was prescribed as it was with men receiving the cat-o'-nine-tails. The fifth and sixth strokes were aimed at the back.

Throughout the proceedings Percy made no sound. Afterwards, the two officers unstrapped the small figure from the table, hustled him through the freezing corridors of Mansfield Bridewell and dumped him in a cell at the back of the police station to serve the rest of his sentence: one day's imprisonment. Twenty-four hours' detention served a double purpose: the weals diminished and, hopefully, penitence increased.

The Mansfield Petty Sessions chairman, Mr W. F. Saunders, and his colleagues, Mr T. Savage, Mr G. H. Hunt and Dr Palmer, had been conscious of acting a mite leniently when sentencing the boy Toplis. Mr Herbert Toplis, his father, had told them that Percy had been a good lad up to six months before, but then 'persons who ought to know better' had brought him to where he was. This first dark allusion to what was to be a life-long preference for unconventional company did not impress the Bench. The chairman suggested somewhat shortly to Mr Toplis that 'there had been some laxity on his part for the boy to have got out of control at eleven years of age'. Six strokes of the birch would suffice, the Bench ruled, along with a strong admonition for father Toplis.

Unfortunately, the case revealed latent tastes and talents in the 11-year-old Toplis that neither birch, nor jail, nor sergeant-major, nor even the battlefields of the First World War itself were to subdue. His crime had been a cool little two-tier confidence trick, providing Percy with both a new suit and 5s. in his pocket. Victim No. 1, Albert Levitt, clothier, of Low Street, Sutton-in-Ashfield, had described to the court how the prisoner had come to his shop and selected two suits of clothes. 'He maintained he had been sent by a Mrs Oscroft of Brook Street, Sutton, and was allowed to take the suits away on approval.' He had then gone along to Mr Alfred Wyeld's pawnbroker shop, impressively rigged out in one of the suits — and had asked for 9s. on the other. Evidently there had been some stiff bargaining, and Percy had settled for 5s.

This initial excursion into a future role of dandy and dare-devil failed through a flaw in planning. Percy had picked on Mrs Oscroft because he knew her to be a credit-worthy citizen of Sutton. Unfortunately, she knew him. Unfortunately, too, for advocates of the short, sharp lesson, the effect on young Percy was fleeting. There were about 2,000 cases of boys below the age of fourteen being birched in Britain that year, and the *News of the World* would later comment about this particular case:

> The corrective influence of the birch rod warmly administered to him by a police court jailer before he had reached the age of twelve failed to check his adventurous disposition ... his overwhelming desire for unnatural excitement and the reckless don't-care-a-hang spirit which was inevitably bound to bring him to an untimely end.
>
> The strong right hand of the law wielding the birch had no deterrent effect.

Three months later, Alderman Johnson Pearson, chairman of the Chesterfield Bench, was listening to another tale of woe. As the local paper headlined it succinctly: 'A Precocious Newsvendor Sold His Papers and Kept the Cash'. Mr Charles Halmshaw, the prosecutor, said that one day he was at the railway station at Shirebrook distributing newspapers to boys when the defendant, Percy Toplis, came up and asked to be taken on. He mentioned the name of a gentleman at the newspaper office and was given thirty-six newspapers to sell. That was the last he had seen of him.

As the court was to discover, Percy Toplis already knew, at the age of 11, which string of the fiddle to pluck.

'My parents have left me, sir,' he told the Bench pathetically. 'I'm living with my grandparents.'

Chairman: 'When did you last see your mother?'

'In Nottingham, sir. I had got the job of carrying a parcel for a lady, and I saw her.'

'Who sent you to Nottingham?'

'No one, sir.'

'And you are only eleven years of age?'

'Yes, sir.'

The chairman appealed to the police-court missioner for help as there seemed to be no one to look after the boy. But eventually Percy's aunt, Annie Webster, appeared. Over the protests of Mr Halmshaw, still complaining that he had not recovered his money, Percy was released on twelve months' probation.

Aunt Annie lived in a one-up, one-down terrace in the shadow of Blackwell pit. There was only a cold tap inside and a closet outside, but there was always a coal fire picked off the tip, and enough to eat. Aunt Annie's husband worked at Blackwell pit and they had no other children to care for. Evidently she had enough of a way with her to keep Percy out of the courts; his talent for trouble was reserved for the teachers at South Normanton Elementary School. At this time Percy still had two years to go before he could legally leave school, as only a Labour Certificate from an employer could release a reluctant scholar before the age of thirteen; and in 1908 there weren't many jobs going for men, let alone boys.

Even in the company of pitmen's sons Percy was a tough character, dominating in the playground and kept in order in class with liberal doses of cane and tawse. But he was popular. 'He had a weird magnetic quality to him, despite his roughness,' recalled one of his classmates, Charles Foulkes. 'He had a strong influence on all

29

of us and got his friends into a lot of scrapes.'

In the autumn of 1909 a new headmaster arrived at South Normanton Elementary, a Mr John Bailey who had ideas on improving the school. He introduced music and singing and occasional expeditions away from the school on nature walks, and he moved his desk into the same room as the senior class so as to keep a close eye on their development. There were even joint play readings with girls from the neighbouring school, where Mr Bailey's wife was headmistress. Then, with Christmas coming up, he proposed a special evening of carols, to include a piano solo from one of the pupils and end with a short closing address. Parents would be invited and it would be a chance to involve them in the life of the school. This rather advanced idea for 1909 required funds, so each teacher was allotted two streets to collect contributions for the concert. Any surplus could be used for a small Christmas gift for the boys. The senior class teacher, Mr Slater, together with Charles Foulkes and a few other boys, set off one night in early December to canvas Downing Street, at the lower end of Mansfield, for whatever small sums, a penny or two, the residents felt inclined to give.

At the first house an elderly lady just shut the door in their faces. Two houses down, a woman shouted, 'Don't be cheeky', and slammed the door. At another house a man said, 'I'm not giving again.' By the time Charles Foulkes met Mr Slater half-way down the street, it had become apparent that they had been thoroughly forestalled, and Mr Slater had moreover discovered who had been there first. The lady at No. 14 happened to know Percy Toplis.

The subsequent drama was played out in full view of the senior class at South Normanton Elementary when Percy walked in through the door the next morning 'as cool as cucumber'. Mr Bailey raged at his desk at the side of the classroom. Witnesses were called. Half-way through the morning the police arrived. Percy Toplis maintained stoutly throughout that his was purely an excess of zeal and his intention simply to do the class's work for it in advance. Finally, 2s. 3½d. was handed over and the concert went ahead — without any further contribution from Percy Toplis.

Percy was duly caned, but by no means cowed. His class teacher, Mr Jack Leary, thin, bronchitic and given only sporadically to bouts of discipline, had two more years of Percy to endure. Another of his schoolmates, Clarence Dudley, remembers a warm summer afternoon in 1911 when Mr Leary was attempting to instil 'the trade-routes of the Empire' into Class 5 standard. Attention was wandering and one of the class actually dozed off, head on one side. Even in one of Mr Leary's less determined moods, this was intolerable. The sleeper was awakened by the swish of a cane. Then, as Mr Leary droned on, the class listened even less. By the end of half an hour the whole class was dozing or asleep and Mr Leary was extracting the truth from one of the more pusillanimous victims.

'Percy Toplis brought in a bottle of laudanum, sir, and passed it round the class, sir.'

The soporific drug had overcome all the pupils. Percy was hauled to the front of the class and bent over a desk. Mr Leary was positioning himself for the first stroke when Percy suddenly lashed out with the most violent backheeler at Mr Leary's shins — and dashed across the classroom, past the headmaster and out of the door.

Mr Bailey yelled after him, 'You'll end your days on the gallows, Percy Toplis, you mark my words.'

As Clarence Dudley remarked, 'It was to prove near enough as a prediction.'

Percy was thus no testament to Mr Bailey's new theories of development. But even at 12 years old he was already an unusual figure: ginger-haired, big for his age, smartly dressed, devoted to his aunt and grandmother, already taking on his friends' fathers at billiards down at the Gladstone Arms — and beating them. Clarence Dudley remembers Toplis as a loner, despite being a dominant figure among his schoolmates:

'A rubber football down at the corner shop cost 6½d. Whenever it burst it was always Percy who went for a new one, and came back with his pockets stuffed with sweets and

31

chocolates. He had a gang of admirers, but he kept all his secrets and went off on his adventures always alone.'

At last, in 1910, at the age of 13, Percy was able to leave school, and Aunt Annie got him a job as an apprentice blacksmith at Blackwell pit where her husband worked. The pay was 1s. 4d. a day. Compared with many of the pits in the Nottinghamshire coalfield, Blackwell was easy-going and reasonably dry, had plenty of room in the gates and a good accident record. But it was hardly the life for the young tearaway of Mansfield.

He was supposed to work on the night shift at Blackwell, but he hardly ever went. There was a quarrel with the pit manager, John Thomas Todd, and words were spoken for which Mr Todd was to suffer an appropriate humiliation a few years later. For the rest of his life, Percy Toplis was to describe his occupation as 'blacksmith', but from now on his only tools were to be his wits. He took off for the north and his first acquaintance with Scotland.

Percy liked the country and found it no problem to turn a penny in its markets and taverns. His piano playing was good enough for the uncritical world of whisky and chasers, his billiards worth a shilling or two and his charm sufficient, even at the age of 14, to ease the problem of lodging. Then, in July at Dumfries, it transpired that he had not paid for two railway tickets for himself and a lady companion: ten days' imprisonment.

A month later he was back in England, making his way through a remote part of Yorkshire, Pateley Bridge in Nidderdale. The tight-fisted Yorkshire folk being less generous in their public houses and more protective of their women, Percy found it necessary to relieve a lady of her purse and £4: one month's hard labour. By the spring of 1912 he was in Lincolnshire and paying court to a young lady. She objected to his attentions and the 15-year-old Toplis was sentenced: two years' hard labour. There was no question of remission, and the young Toplis was left to contemplate the approach of the First World War — and with it his destiny — behind the gates of Lincoln Jail.

4

Even in January the climate in Malta is rarely unpleasant: odd chill days, some rain, but nothing untoward to mar one of the most pleasant billets to be had in that middle year of the First World War, 1916.

But Private George Ward, RAMC, stationed with Military Hospital Company No. 1, was scarcely counting his luck. In the three months he had been in Malta he had been bathing once, and into the alluring citadel of Valletta not at all. The army took the view that there was a war on, and frivolous indulgence in matters of rest and recreation were not to be encouraged. Walking the corridors of the rather draughty Malta General Military Hospital, Private Ward reflected that there was more life back home in No. 49 Colliery Row, Mansfield, than there was in exotic Malta. At least, back home, the Miners' Club and a pint of Nottingham mild ale were just down the road.

Even the work was something less than glamorous: a tiny trickle of sick and wounded from Salonika on the Balkan Front, occasional accidents among the garrison, VD, of course, odd transfers from ships on their way out to obscure campaigns in Mesopotamia.

Private Ward was desultorily changing the bandages of

an artillery man who had lost a finger in a gun-breech accident, when an immaculately dressed officer came striding down the 'other ranks' ward towards him. The man was in the full-dress uniform of a major, boots gleaming, cap nonchalantly under his left arm, and a clutch of medal ribbons on his chest.

'Ward, old chap. Got you a leave pass for tonight.'

Private Ward looked up to recognize his old neighbour from No. 52 Colliery Row, Mansfield.

That night the bizarre twosome of a private and a major, both of them in full army uniform, sampled a reasonable cross-section of bars in the Gut, ventured as far as the back streets of Sliema, and roared with laughter at how easy it was to baffle the British Army if only you were dressed as an officer and a gentleman.

Percy Toplis had emerged from Lincoln Jail in the midst of the patriotic hysteria of late 1914. White feathers, Lord Kitchener and the swagger of uniformed friends had moved him little. But when 1915 came round and there was talk of conscription and little hope of peace, Percy decided valour was the better part of discretion and volunteered for the army. Summer found him amid a familiar unlovely land-scape: litters of slag heaps, pithead winding gear, squat miners' cottages — the battlefield of Loos, archetype for all the scenes that were to follow of unconscionable sacrifices and imperceptible gain. Private Francis Percy Toplis, RAMC, was detailed for stretcher-bearing duties behind the first wave at Loos.

The chaos and confusion of Loos cured Percy of any smear of patriotic fervour once and for all. It was the first gas attack by the British on the Germans. Most of the gas drifted limply out of the crude cylinders in the front line and back into the British trenches; the wire of the German lines was left almost intact by the inadequate artillery barrage. When a breach was made and the first German line taken, the reserve troops had been left too far back and failed to exploit the advantage. Percy, toiling away under fire to extract some of the daunting mass of 15,000 casualties, saw nothing to ease his contempt for the unimaginative General Staff who had contrived this fiasco. General Douglas Haig, commanding one of the Loos armies, and Private Percy Toplis, stretcher-bearer, each then determined that, for them, there would never be a repetition.

Haig, who had fumed helplessly for three days waiting for adequate reinforcements to exploit what he thought to be a chance of a breakthrough, immediately began scheming to depose his Commander-in-Chief in France, Sir John French. Percy Toplis contrived leave on the compassionate grounds that his non-existent wife had died in childbirth.

Haig wrote a sinuous letter denouncing French to Lord Kitchener, following it up with a conspiratorial lunch with Lord Haldane, the War Minister, and even managing a few words of vitriol to George V himself when the king visited France. This first campaign of Haig's was more brilliant and successful than, if equally as muddy as, any of his subsequent battles in the field. Within three months Haig was invited by the Prime Minister, Mr Asquith, to be Commander-in-Chief of the forces in France. By that time Private Toplis was in England on the only official spell of leave he was to have in his entire life.

As the darkened locomotive pulled out of St Pancras Station, Percy Toplis settled back secure in the knowledge that his exploits at Loos would not be underestimated by his admirers back home. It had not been difficult to remove a captain's uniform from the sad detritus of the clearing station behind the Loos lines. Persuading Hawkes & Co., Military and Civilian Outfitters of Savile Row, to grant a gallant officer a small credit on a new dress uniform was child's play to a fellow who had tried his very first confidence trick on a tailor at the age of 11. But the Distinguished Conduct Medal had been a more subtle stroke. Its coveted ribbon sat well above his left pocket; an at once discreet but unmistakable badge of heroism, and an unspoken rebuke to any who might detect the slightest hint of an East Midland

35

accent or pit-village manners beneath the polished Sam Browne belt and the gleaming riding-boots. The bandage on his left knee was an insurance policy with the RAMC professional touch, just tight enough to produce a limp. A wounded officer would be immune.

Toplis need not have worried. Blackwell colliery had found its first decorated, wounded, home-grown hero, who had made it to a commission too. The very first night the colliery manager, John Thomas Todd, so far forgot the profit of his coal-owner and his own past quarrels with Toplis as to order up champagne for a toast at the Miners' Club. Ralph Ward, George Ward's nephew, from two doors up in Colliery Row, vividly remembers the handsome young charlatan accepting the glass of bubbly as though it had been his constant refreshment in the brief intervals between his glorious feats of arms. As the night wore on, and the champagne was transmuted into plainer beer, the members of Blackwell Colliery Miners' Club became familiar with the intrepid but hopeless assault on Hill 70; the curtain of Boche machine-gun fire which had mown down the 24th Division in row after row; the diffident account of Captain Toplis's encounter with a German pill-box; the lone return, through God's good grace, with two wounded men, ten prisoners and a bullet wound in the knee to show for it.

Mr Todd made a gruff but affecting speech and invited the colliery's most celebrated man to drill the local volunteers the following day. Toplis, when he woke up, dressed carefully for a visit to Mansfield's only professional photographer. More than sixty years on, the portrait of the dashing captain still stares out in discreet confidence, a picture of a man sure of his background and role in life. The photographer put the picture on a little easel in his window with a carefully hand-printed notice, 'Captain Percy Toplis, DCM, of Mansfield', and sent a copy to the *Nottingham Evening Post*. It would be five years before it was to be printed — and then as a picture of 'The Most Wanted Man in Britain'.

The evening of the great Blackwell Local Defence

36

Volunteers' drill in honour of Percy Toplis is a treasured memory to this day among those who had the privilege to see it. Ernest Leah met the hero and conducted him to the Blackwell Cricket Club ground:

'He told us that he had been wounded on active service and that he was on sick leave. We believed his story, of course, about the wound, and he was given a chair from which to do his drilling. I can remember it as if it was yesterday, [him] sitting there about where the umpire usually stood.'

It was a motley crew which marched on to the field to greet the ceremonial drillmaster. Most wore their pit boots, the nurtured turf of the outfield having been willingly sacrificed to the exigencies of war. The odd khaki jacket was worn, acquired from returning relatives, and even, on this distinguished occasion, two full-dress uniforms with medals adorning two middle-aged Boer War veterans. They had both had their day at Ladysmith and drunk off it for fifteen years. But even they were subdued by the aura of more present dangers. Each man carried the long wooden handle used on miners' shovels.

Toplis started gently. 'Order arms. Stand at ease.' (Page three of the *Infantry Training Manual*, 1914.) Not a flicker of inappropriate amusement as a man in the middle row promptly dropped his shovel handle.

'Atten-shun. Slope arms. By the right, dress. Form, fours.'

Fully half a minute of hopeless muttering and muddle as the military men sorted themselves out. Ralph Ward got a shovel handle in the eye, but thought better of complaining in the presence of a veteran of Hill 70.

'Right turn. Quick march.' Toplis sent them away towards the square-leg boundary. 'Left wheel.'

Away they went across the far end of the ground against the skyline dominated by the main Blackwell colliery spoil heap.

'Left wheel. Left wheel,' again. And then, 'Halt,' in front of the seated hero.

37

It was only now that the celebrated 18-year-old drill-master realized that his two old foes were tucked away in the rear rank. And a night of champagne was not sufficient to anaesthetize the memories they brought back, or to buy off the months of victimization. As Ernest Leah remembers:

'Percy reckoned his old boss, the mine manager, Todd, and the under-manager, Johnson, had given him a hard time as a lad, so he singled them out for some very hard drilling that night.'

'Attention. Slope arms. About turn. Halt. Present arms.'

Inevitably, Toplis's two victims, like most of their colleagues, were hopelessly behind.

'Step forward, Todd and Johnson.' Flushed with the indignity of it all, the two managers took a pace out of the line. 'Left turn, quick march, halt, slope arms, present arms, about turn.' Toplis forced the unhappy pair into a ragged demonstration of the entire army drill-book. Finally, like a ringmaster with the big cats, he ordered, 'Attack position. Down.'

Ernest Leah counted silently to twenty while the rulers of Blackwell lay prostrate in front of the new khaki khan from Colliery Row:

'Then he made them run round the ground till they were exhausted. Percy, of course, was laughing his head off all the time.'

One evening had paid off a clutch of old scores.

King for a week at home, Percy Toplis left Mansfield determined that the real British Army would likewise bend a little more to his will. At the very least, France, its mud and its blood, was definitely out.

At that time in 1915, the newspapers were happily diverting their readers away from the unglamorous carnage across the Channel to the exotic tale of a triumphant little 'side-show' half the world away in Mesopotamia, or what is now Iraq. Major-General Townshend, replete with pig-sticking cavalry and the crack regiments of the Indian Army, was rolling up the dastardly Turks along the banks of the River Tigris. There had been a splendid old-fashioned victory in

38

North-West Frontier style at Amara, and the papers carried tales of the troops basking in the sun and enjoying unspecified oriental delights in the bazaars of Basra and the Persian Gulf. To Toplis it seemed a sufficient contrast to Mademoiselle of Armentières and December in the trenches. It was fortunate for him that he only got as far as Malta and his night out with Private Ward before the news came through of General Townshend's defeat, his surrender at Kut, and a four-week march of degradation and death across the desert to a Turkish prison camp.

The troop-ship turned round and returned to England. In future, 'side-shows' would have to take second place to the immutable collision on the Western Front.

Toplis returned in early 1917 to an England of bitterness and unrest, of strikes by the police and engineers, of one Member of Parliament, Sir John Jackson, caught out collecting £80,000 a year for himself through inflated contracts to the War Office, and of another, W. C. Anderson, demanding conscription of wealth and property to match conscription of men. Anderson's fellow socialists, hot with the news from Russia, were planning a conference of the Second International in Stockholm to try and stop the war. While 20 million men endured the winter of 1916-17 in trenches the length of Europe, the newspaper *The Call* wrote:

The nations are still pursuing the insensate path for race suicide. The insatiable war machine still shatters and annihilates with a fiendish regularity. Whole battalions of fathers and brothers, enter the inferno and melt away like summer snow. Our streets are filled with the halt and the blind. A load of sorrow is accumulating in every home in the land.

Yet London continued to flaunt the delights of peacetime. The horse-racing fixtures continued, the clubs stayed open. Private Toplis, back from Malta and facing the inevitable return to France, once again got out his hero's regalia and adjourned to the metropolis. Years later, after his spectacular death, an acquaintance remembered the consummate actor who had fooled them all in wartime 'society', and reminisced profitably about him to the *World's Pictorial News*:

'He would walk along the Strand with the air of a man with an important mission. I was with him one day when he stopped suddenly, turned round with a military air, and called out "Corporal." The non-com he addressed walked back. "Why didn't you salute me?" asked Toplis in an imperious manner. "I didn't see you, sir," replied the man, saluting. Toplis, with a wave of his stick, snapped out "Then keep your eyes open in future, corporal," and passed on. I never saw anything done more properly. Not a shadow of doubt concerning the bona fides of the officer could have entered the non-com's mind. I certainly had none.'

The newspaper continued:

At this time Toplis was 'carrying on' in the West End. And he was 'carrying on' with a vengeance. To have heard him talk one would have believed him to have been a veritable hero.

He was a frequent visitor at a house in Maida Vale — a house that stands in its own grounds, and is owned by a wealthy clay merchant. The lady of the establishment was strongly 'smitten' by the charms of the 'noble and gallant' British officer who had achieved so much. She introduced him to her daughters and he took them out for motor rides and to theatres. The tale that he told her was that he had been trained at the Camberley School for Officers, from which he went out to India, and came back for the war. He further stated that he was the only son of a retired army general, who had fallen out with him, and that he found it necessary for the present to 'exist' on his pay. The name which served him on this occasion was Major Williams, and he frequently declared his intention of 'going back to France and winning his spurs'.

There was none who knew better than he the art of disguise. He was fully as skilled and adept as Charles Peace, whom he copied in many ways. Then he always went about fully armed. Once at a London night club he had a dispute at cards and drew a revolver, which he declared he was quite prepared to use. He terrified everyone, and one man afterwards described him as 'a fellow who stood with tilted chin and blazing eyes, the very picture of animated fury'.

Again, in a house off the Euston Road, when challenged by a man who threatened to rob him, he fired two shots at a mirror which stood over the mantelpiece. Indeed, there never was a time when he was not prepared to shoot.

The boy from Blackwell was now just 19, and doing well. But though he had been absent without leave for weeks on end, he was not yet ready to risk the firing squad and to desert his unit. The assembled might of military justice still seemed a formidable deterrent, the twin sirens of 'society' and 'socialism' not yet loud enough for him to dare everything. All that was to change in March 1917. And it was the vast British Army base camp at Étaples in France, later his scene of triumph, which was first to be his education.

Despite his truancy, the army considered a draft to France sufficient retribution for his absence without leave. Toplis and his detachment of the RAMC marched the twenty miles from Boulogne to Étaples through a doleful and unbroken colonnade: hospitals, cemeteries, prisoner-of-war camps — sentinels of death, signposts to the fate that awaited the new detachments.

At Étaples, however, he found a new tense and aggrieved atmosphere among the 20,000 troops. The lingering, subservient, patriotic acceptance of the crusade against the Boche which Toplis had known at Loos had given way to mere endurance of a war that might not only not end wars, but would, apparently, never end itself. On the first day there he saw Australians rampaging through the camp after a drinking bout, insulting the Military Police and cutting free the victims of field punishment, tied to gun wheels by their wrists. In the Salvation Army hut there was talk of front-line pacts with the Germans. One story from the Somme told of a sentries' truce: 'We were in a sap,' went the tale, 'with a German observation post only five to six yards away when we heard some shouts of, "English, English." We talked and agreed to a form of armistice — so we shot to the right and they to the left.'

And then there was a seductive encounter with a deserter, brazenly queueing up for his food from the hospital mess: 'Oh, there's dozens of us round here. They haven't got a clue who's real and who isn't. There's food on tap, plenty of blokes with money in their pockets, and always a chance of wriggling your way back on a boat to Blighty.'

Astonished, Toplis learned that there were whole communities of deserters in the woods and sand-dunes between Étaples and the once genteel watering place of Le Touquet.

'They make a few sorties, but they hardly ever catch anyone. Safest place is right here in the camp, of course. Providing you're carrying a chit of paper!'

When, in March 1917, Private Toplis left Étaples for the doomed attack at Arras, he was already set on a new and extraordinary path which was to lead him to challenge the invisible panoply of the British Army, its caste system and tradition, and ultimately to threaten even its ability to launch one of the great battles of the war.

5

The man who was to confront, and be crushed by, Percy Toplis, had had all the privilege and protection denied to his adversary. Brigadier-General Andrew Graham Thomson, Royal Engineers, Commandant of the base camp at Étaples, France, had been privately educated by tutors and moulded by the manners of mid-Victorian England. Where Toplis had been reared by the poverty of the coal-fields, tempered by his clashes with authoritarian justice in Nottinghamshire, and taught resource and resilience in the tempestuous years before the outbreak of the war, Thomson had sailed almost untroubled through the sheltered waters of an army officer's career in that gallant era when the Empire was at its zenith.

In appearance, character and background, Thomson was not unlike his commander, Field-Marshal Haig. He had the same full-moustached, implacable expression. Like his Commander-in-Chief, he sprang from a Scottish upper-class family and displayed the same quality of stubbornness and inflexibility. Like Haig, he had served as a junior officer in the South African War, where it was so often said that the British Army consisted of lions led by donkeys. And he shared his commander's love of the cavalry. But of the working classes, who were to form the bulk of the soldiers under his command in France in 1917, he knew almost nothing.

From the sympathetic obituary written about him in the *Royal Engineers Journal* of June 1926, it is evident that, next to officers and horses, Thomson had, earlier in his life, been most at ease with natives. The obituary, or memoir as it was called, was, inevitably, written by a fellow general, Sir Elliot Wood, KCB. It is almost silent about Thomson's service in the First World War, saying only that he had to come home after a serious breakdown in health, but is by contrast fulsome about his early career. The memoir reads:

He was commissioned, R.E., in January, 1877.

In 1879, as 1st Lieut., he joined the 17th Fortress Company at Aldershot and proceeded to Malta the following year, where he made his mark in work and sports.

He was one of the R.E. officers' team which beat the combined garrison at football, and one of the three 17th Co. officers who beat all comers at Water Polo. He became a useful polo player, and had an uncommonly good barb which he ran in the races.

Sir Elliot then lists a roll-call of the obscure glories of Queen Victoria's soldiers: the Egyptian campaign of 1882, the skirmishes at Hasheen and Tai Mai, the victory under Sir Garnet Wolseley at Tel el-Kebir, the Suakin campaign in the Sudan.

The enemy were all around Suakin, and Thomson's company had to look out for itself. Here he was equally as successful with the native labour parties as he was with the Egyptian.

On returning to Suakin from home in June, 1885, a crowd of Thomson's old working parties clustered round him with every manifestation of delight at seeing him again — and, indeed, they had a name of their own for him.

Mentioned in Despatches, gaining a clasp, Thomson received the brevet of Major for his services, immediately on his being promoted Captain.

It is an almost idyllic picture of the dashing empire-builder. But 'uncommonly good barb' horses and a way with native labour were to prove poor accoutrements when, at the age of 59, it came to a contest with the tough young champion of new politics and old resentments. And such lessons as the army had taught Andrew Graham Thomson were to make him even more aloof and inflexible, ill-suited material to face the fury of the new soldiers.

For Thomson's career had begun to go wrong nine years before. In September 1908 he had been given the coveted job of Commandant of the Royal Military Academy at Woolwich, and the rank of full colonel to go with it. It was near enough to London to keep his gregarious wife Annie in touch with London society, and close enough to the War Office to keep them cognisant of his talents. Best of all, Thomson could play the experienced, heroic but warm-hearted father-figure to his young officer cadets. There is no doubt that he was respected, even held in affection, by his cadets.

The Thomsons threw parties and entertained widely. Within two months of her arrival at Woolwich, Annie Thomson was the star of the academy's play *Our Boys*, and won a rave review: 'The hit of the evening was the rendering by Mrs Thomson, the wife of the Commandant, as Belinda, the loyal little lodging house slave.' Her husband, too, basked in the company of these young cadets, mostly themselves sons of officers and 'gentlemen'.

During the long, hot summer of 1911, he issued the unprecedented order that parades could be held in shirt-sleeves. He generally relaxed discipline, sponsored end-of-term dances and encouraged the Academy's dramatic society.

But after three halcyon years at Woolwich, Thomson received, out of the blue, a mortifying public rebuke from which he was never to recover. The British Army too were to suffer for the few harsh words spoken that summer's day in 1911. No less a person than the Chief of the Imperial General Staff, Sir John French, had come down for open day at 'The Shop', as Woolwich was known. And suddenly, in the midst of the expected speech of platitudes about the loyalty and patriotism expected from the cadets, Sir John launched into a fierce attack on the conduct and discipline of 'Shop' pupils. With Thomson standing beside him, he demanded a return to proper standards of dress, more drill, an end to the hectic social life at Woolwich, and less leave.

The wounds of this onslaught went deep enough to be remembered even a generation later when the history of the Woolwich Academy came to be written. And the effect on Thomson was traumatic. Never again would he permit himself the smallest sympathetic indulgence for the troops under his command, nor the slightest deviation from King's Regulations.

Before long, Thomson was replaced as commandant at Woolwich. He consoled himself in the company of family and old friends. His brother-in-law, Major Addison Yalden Thomson of the Cameronians, was a former tea planter in India, a director of several public companies and a master of hounds with a large estate at Thorncombe, Crowcombe, near Taunton. He also owned a small island off the northern shores of Scotland. Although Thomson owned a sixteen-room house in London, 72 St George's Square, Westminster, and was a member of the Junior United Services Club, he spent most of his time with the major, riding and hunting.

Members of the family of Major Yalden Thomson are still alive, and retain memories of those long-ago house parties when they were children. They called Thomson 'Old Chips' because of his flinty personality. They also remember that though they never met him, they had a cousin known as 'Young Chips', whose portrait hung on the drawing-room wall. The family snapshots show Yalden Thomson and Thomson together in the group of officers taken at

46

Warminster Barracks, and the husband-and-wife team boating and picnicking together.

The Yalden Thomson governess, 93-year-old Hildred Vose, living on the Isle of Wight, distinctly remembers Old Chips:

'A very forbidding, even rather terrifying, and certainly not a very talkative, man.'

She cannot remember that he ever referred to Young Chips, but there does exist one very faded, sepia-brown photograph taken in the Orkneys in which Thomson looks relaxed, and though unsmiling, is to be seen gazing lovingly across the picnic hampers at a handsome-looking young man. Young Chips, his only child, was in fact killed early in the war while serving as a junior officer. This was a personal tragedy which so embittered Thomson that he forbade his wife ever to speak about it.

The profession of arms which had served Thomson well until he was past fifty years old had turned to gall. It was to make him a brittle adversary for the young man who had shifted so artfully for himself in those years in the coalfields of Nottinghamshire.

6

In the early days of September 1917, the British Army was preparing for its own special Calvary: the assault on a tiny hump of Flanders soil known as Passchendaele Ridge.

Already the weather had turned. General Thomson at Étaples recorded the 'terrible storms' which blew down the tented hospitals. Two thousand eight hundred and thirty-one beds were put out of use, and nurses were tending to the wounded in the wind and the rain. On the Ypres front, vast expanses of mud were keeping the supply columns strictly to the Menin Road and corralling them at Hell Fire Corner under an endless cascade of comfortably calibrated shells from the German guns. A mere quarter of a million men were to fall in that all-enveloping quagmire within the next two months, less than half the number of casualties that the Somme had exacted a year before. Yet Passchendaele was to be remembered even more bitterly for the futility of its attacks, for the apparently effortless impregnability of the German pill-boxes, and above all for the special horrors of that distinctive mud: mud as soft and bottomless as quicksand, and as quickly lethal; liquid which filled up the shell-holes and seeped into the trenches as fast as water into a child's diggings on an English beach. The battle imposed the most agonized trials of endurance. Even today the memories are sharp-edged in the correspondence of Étaples veterans who went on to fight there.

'I lay from Thursday morning until Sunday afternoon in a shell-hole with a shattered leg, up to my neck in muddy water, until some lads from the Manchesters got me out' — Ted Asher of Lincoln.

'I was buried all but my head and shoulders after a shell blast. The Germans passed over me three times before I was picked up two days later' — Peter Sanson of Birmingham.

By November, only three miles had been gained. 'A victory without sweets,' Colonel Seton Hutchinson called it. 'The enemy gave only a crumbling mud honeycomb filled with a sticky gaseous slime.' Mostly the enemy gave nothing at all. Stories of futile heroism were legion. The Royal Warwicks found themselves being slaughtered with nonchalant ease by shirt-sleeved Prussians in front of Polderhoek Château. For two days they were pinned down, waiting for relief, or at the very least food. On the third night a captain from the 14th Warwicks arrived with neither food nor relief; only orders to attack again. As one of the Warwicks, H. V. Drinkwater, recalled in one of those vivid, bitter little stories which epitomize Passchendaele:

'Our subaltern pointed out with all eloquence the impossibility of our men again attacking. What was left of our men could hardly stand. Whilst agreeing, the 14th captain nevertheless had orders to carry out the attack. They sat in the pill-box, both covered in mud — clothes, hands and faces. By the light of a candle it was apparent how much each felt his responsibility. At daybreak the captain walked out of the pill-box and along a trench. He was sniped in the head. It was bravely done. He knew that trench was exposed. The attack never took place.'

Passchendaele was to become the symbol of the First World War's endless sacrifice and aimless attrition. But to Field-Marshal Douglas Haig it was far from futile. Passchendaele, for him, met both public policy and private

49

obsession. Throughout the late winter and early spring, 'that man of gun-metal', as one of his commanders described Haig, had suffered in inarticulate indignation through a series of humiliations.

Lloyd George, the new Prime Minister, who hated Haig, had sent out a special commission led by General Smuts to visit the Flanders armies. Its instructions were to comb through the commanders in the field for a successor to this man Haig, whose sole strategy seemed to be to buy German blood with British blood, drop for drop. The mission failed. Despondently, Smuts and Milner trawled the staff quarters, Gough, Rawlinson, Plumer. But all seemed hypnotized by the black angel of attrition: Gough, who had seen his Fifth Army flounder to a standstill in 1916; Plumer, who was too cautious even for Haig; Rawlinson, who had for a moment dared to propose an imaginative flight of strategy for the Somme battle. None had suggested to Milner or Smuts that they had any alternative to the monotonous collision of flesh against machine-gun bullets, the direct assaulting of wire, concrete, wire, pill-boxes and more wire by men with rifle and bayonet.

But Lloyd George, who thought the war could be won in the Balkans, or in Italy, or on the sea — anywhere but along the 350 miles of immense defensive fortifications between Switzerland and Zeebrugge — was not to be denied. When Haig came to London in January 1917, it was clear to Lloyd George that he was planning another Somme. With the doleful collusion of Admiral Jellicoe and the dour support of 'Wullie' Robertson, Chief of the Imperial General Staff, Haig stuck to his plans. There would, for a third time, be a battle of Ypres. It was certain that Germany was crumbling. Victory was assured. In that year, 1917, Lloyd George, the amateur strategist, raged but could make no headway against the united front of the military men and the enfilade from General Smuts, his colleague in the War Cabinet.

Then the French suddenly produced a man after Lloyd George's own heart in General Nivelle, the hero of Verdun, who was appointed to replace Joffre in command of the

French armies. Quick-talking, bilingual, charming, dynamic, Nivelle came to London with a bold, inventive plan to break the deadlock on the Western Front, and Lloyd George was captivated to the point where he determined to give Nivelle total support and buckle the intransigent Haig to his plan. On a chilly night at Calais in February, Lloyd George confronted Haig with a secret decision of the British War Cabinet to place him and his armies under Nivelle's command. Haig, rigid with indignation, and, as usual, at a loss for words, retreated to his room to gather himself for a fight. But there was no way out other than resignation of his command, which was not Haig's way. So from February through March, April and May, Haig suffered the cock-sure insolent instructions of Nivelle, endured the private humiliation. 'It is a type of letter which no gentleman could have drafted and it is also one which certainly no Commander-in-Chief of this great British Army should receive without protest,' he complained to his diary after a particularly peremptory note from Nivelle, but Haig was confident that in the end Nivelle's plans would fail and his own time would come.

That day arrived on 16 April 1917, with immense conse-quences for Haig, for the new conscript British Army, for Percy Toplis, already a deserter, and for General Thomson, worrying principally about the absence of an officers' venereal hospital at Étaples. The whole of Haig's strategy for the rest of 1917, the third battle of Ypres, his response to trouble from his own troops, was to be dominated by the disasters of that day.

At dawn on that 16 April, the French Army went over the top along the Aisne against the enemy which had for over a month had full knowledge of their plans, and which had retreated to the most impregnable of all its defensive works — the Hindenburg Line. By evening of the second day, Nivelle had lost 120,000 men. Nowhere had he penetrated further than two miles. Haig, engaged in a diversionary operation up at Arras with 29,000 killed, watched with grim rectitude the collapse of the arrogant Frenchman and his chimera of the dramatic and sudden breakthrough. By 28 April, Nivelle was dismissed and disgraced. Lloyd George could do nothing and the chalice passed to Haig. But it was already poisoned. For as Nivelle left the battlefield, insulted and screamed at in a final showdown with his own commanders, the French Army mutinied.

The stories which Haig heard from his new colleague, General Pétain, were to be burned into his mind and dominate his own reactions when, five months later, his own army was faced with refusals of orders, violence and open mutiny. Haig's mutiny was to stay a total secret. The French mutiny of 1917, too, remains an extraordinary fragmented and veiled story. Certainly it seems to have begun when on 3 May a group of black colonial troops refused to go into the line. Several men were arrested and shot out of hand. The regiment, the 21st Division of Colonial Infantry, went back into action and was virtually wiped out in front of the German pill-boxes. But the German machine-gunners had not erased the French Command's difficulties. Over the next two months the generals of the French High Command were to see the flower of their army collapse into mutiny. Seventy-eight regiments revolted. Rebellion spread the whole length of the front from Flanders to distant Savoy, 300 miles away on the Swiss frontiers, and the war was on the point of being lost. The French military authorities were in consternation. Like the British, they had no policy for dealing with mutiny and rebellion other than mass execution. But the new Commander, Pétain, agonizing over death sentences by night, touring division after division by day, attempted to stem the tide. He came to learn by heart the names of the agitators who were spreading the opium message of peace among his troops: Orieux, Jalina, Didier, Duval back in Paris, Globa with the Russians in Champagne. The government of France was to be reminded again that grievance and suffering could produce men capable of confronting the entire authority of the nation. And in the doctrines of socialism and Bolshevism, pouring out of Russia since the February Revolution three months before, were texts and to spare.

At Coeuvres, only fifty miles from Paris, two French regiments set out for the capital, armed to the teeth, intent on forcing the government to stop the war. The trouble had spread from the great railway junction at Soissons where troops had beaten up a brigadier, stoned the commandant's headquarters, attacked every officer who showed his face, and broken open the prison camp to free all their comrades from detention. (The British Army's own mutiny would later open in an almost identical way.) The fever in the French Army then spread to the Third Corps in camp ten miles from Soissons. Frenzied mass meetings sucked in the whole of two regiments. Even junior officers joined in. Then, amid tumultuous shouting, the men voted to march to Paris.

In a long convoy of lorries they set out from camp. Three military policemen who tried to intervene were strung up from the trees. An army doctor showed his face. He was beaten up and left at the side of the road. The mob, full of French wine and Dutch courage, milled into the railway sidings at Soissons, waving red flags and singing 'The Internationale'. Conveniently, a battered locomotive was waiting there with steam up and a string of empty carriages — the next leave train for the Gare du Nord. Within minutes the driver found himself converted into the vanguard of an armed advance on Paris. Cautiously he edged the mobile mutiny down the track towards the capital. With troops lying on the carriage roofs and riding shotgun on the steps, the train made slow progress under the first low bridge two miles down the line. For a few moments there were the startled faces of new recruits as another train passed slowly enough to pick up the shouts of, 'Stop the War. Join us in Paris.'

In fits and starts the train rumbled fifteen miles south to the junction at Villers—Cotterets. The driver explained incessantly the idiosyncrasies of steam traction. Another bend came up and the mutineers urged him on. They would see the Gare du Nord by nightfall. The train built up speed. Suddenly there were shrieks of warning. The driver

53

snatched for the brake and the train clattered to a halt yards short of a pile of boulders and tree-trunks piled across the line. There was a moment's silence. Then from the thick cover at either side of the line came the familiar tattoo of machine-gun bullets. The initial burst skimmed the heads of the men on the top of the carriages, and another moment of silence followed. Then came an order from the ground, 'Put down your arms and surrender.' Meekly, the 36th and 129th Regiments of Infantry shuffled down off the train and out of the revolution. The loyalist cavalry who had ambushed them never had to lower the sights of their machine-guns. The mutineers marched sheepishly back to Soissons, to face the front again or the firing squad.

Three days later, two men heard the first full details of the developing mutiny: Field-Marshal Sir Douglas Haig and Private Percy Toplis. For Haig, it was a guarded but authentic account at his headquarters from General Pétain's chief of staff himself. For Toplis, in his bivouac on the Somme, it was a vivid and personal story from three French deserters. For Haig, discreet and unsurprised, it was another onerous burden on his great Passchendaele project. For Toplis, it was a moment of illumination. The first day of the battle of Arras, back in April, had finally convinced Toplis that there was for him no future in the war: snow, sleet, rain, the apparently impassable Siegfried Line, the drift of gas from British shells, the deadly game of musical chairs for a seat on Vimy Ridge, the gruesome remnants he carried back to the clearing stations ... Private Percy Toplis, RAMC, decided that enough was enough. One night in the middle of April he melted away to join one of the most bizarre of all the brotherhoods of the First World War.

Skulking, starving, marauding — but surviving — a numberless regiment of deserters was holed up on the old abandoned battlefield of the Somme away to the south. Germans, French, English, Belgians, they lived in uneasy comradeship in the hulks of command posts, old pill-boxes and battered trenches. The war had moved on from that most terrible of all killing grounds and left its own armistice.

Occasionally sweeps of Haig's cavalry quartered the waste-
land. From odd dugouts men were flushed out and harrassed
back to the prison cages and courts martial. But through the
winter and spring of 1917 the army of deserters grew. When
Toplis arrived he found an almost military discipline. Food
was stolen by roster. There was sentry duty against the
cavalry. The talk was of the war, but even more of the great
revolution.

To this international company there came in early June
1917 a new draft of French recruits with a tale to tell of
which neither the German High Command nor the British
Government had yet heard a whisper. The French Army was
refusing to fight. Reinforcements going to the front were
baaing like lambs going to the slaughter. A machine-gun
corps had overthrown its officers and set off for a munitions
factory with guns mounted on lorries. Two regiments had
held out for a week, entrenched in their own lines for all the
world as if it were Verdun, and surrounded by cavalry. They
surrendered, but the revolution spread, to the colonials,
territorials, even to the crack Chasseurs Alpins. And at the
centre of it all was the siren propaganda of the new socialism — leaflets, newspapers, tracts and the furtive oratory of
a new Left flourishing, by official complaisance, in the
boulevards of Paris.

From General Debeney, Pétain's chief of staff, Haig
heard the official story. With just seven days to go to his
great assault on the Messines Ridge, he learned that the
French Army was out of the fight. There could be no more
attacks. It was even extremely doubtful if the defensive line
could be held. The British would have to attack alone.
Indeed, they must attack if the weight was to be taken off
the French Army. Debeney kept from Haig the appalling
statistics. And Haig kept the news from the British Government. But the French Chamber of Deputies heard it all in
secret session: fifty-four divisions of the French Army were
affected, 21,000 men had deserted, only two reliable
divisions remained between the Germans and Paris.

Retribution had been severe, the firing squad accounted

for dozens of men, there was summary execution in the field, even the literal and merciless use of the ancient Roman decimation: one man in every ten ordered to step forward and then be led away to his death. A whole battalion of 200 men or more was marched away into no-man's-land and shelled by its own artillery. To Haig, soldier from the class of 1884, it was the most chilling of news. If the Germans heard of it, if they were given any respite, the whole war might be lost. From those sunny days of early June to the chill of November, the British fought because the French could not fight. And fought on because Haig was certain his troops could be pushed on for ever if need be in the great game of attrition. It was unthinkable that the British soldier might collapse into rebellion or resistance like the Frenchman.

When the day of 9 September 1917 came to shatter the field-marshal's confidence, it was at a most crucial juncture in his prosecution of the war. The plan was to capture the Passchendaele Ridge, from which the Allied armies had been bombarded by the Germans for more than two years. The ridge hunched its back on the horizon four miles from the pinched British front line around the battered town of Ypres. Its capture might be some reward for the blood of another sterile and demoralizing year of war. But the initial attack had drowned in four days of unseasonable downpour in early August, and the line had moved barely a mile. Yet Haig, in a miasma of self-delusion, thought a breakthrough was near: 'A large proportion of the enemy troops are reported to have run away,' he said in a dispatch from a front which had inflicted 30,000 casualties on his men in four days. He ordered General Plumer to attack again towards Passchendaele.

Plumer had watched the creeping disillusion of the conscript British Army. By 9 September he knew that the nine divisions of British and Australians that Haig had provided for him would hardly suffice. It was to be attrition again, and every man was needed. Along the Ypres to Menin Road were gathered dismounted cavalry, re-formed regiments, returned wounded, any man who could be rustled up to trade his life for a German. That day, too, the French were engaged in a strange and bloody exercise, but far from the front line. For the fearful consequences of sedition which Haig and Pétain alike had cause to dread had come to pass. Mutiny had given the spark to insurrection. Ten thousand troops of France's Russian allies, serving in Champagne, had overthrown their officers, set up soviets and declared a Bolshevik revolution. Now they were surrounded by French cavalry, artillery and three brigades of infantry. Thousands of miles from home, but buoyed up by propaganda from Trotsky and his friends in Paris, and the bewitching oratory of Private Globa, the Russians refused to surrender.

As the mutiny at Étaples unfolded victoriously through the middle days of September, simultaneously the new Bolsheviks of Champagne were systematically shelled into defeat by the heavy artillery of the French Army, but only after three days and nights of machine-gunning and trench warfare a hundred miles behind the front line. Some weeks earlier, Private Percy Toplis too had made his dispositions. He had made his way from the ragged company on the Somme back to the old familiar territory of Étaples where his talents for bluff and disguise would allow him a more elegant life. It was a journey which was to threaten the British Army with that same plague which had brought such mortal danger to France.

7

On a low rise overlooking the Channel coast of France south of Boulogne stands one of the largest of all British war cemeteries. Rolling endlessly through sparse trees, couch-grass and shrubs, the graves of 11,000 men straggle away up the road towards Boulogne. Étaples is the cruellest of cemeteries. Here lie the men who died lingeringly of gas and gangrene, without limbs or sight — the pitiful roll-call of those who lived long enough to endure the stretcher journey back through darkness and mud and shell-fire to the clearing stations, who survived the rattling cattle wagons with bunks stacked three or four high, who faced the surgeon and the operating table, but who could not hold on to life long enough to see England again. They were buried by the professional mourners from the military hospital, ten, fifteen, twenty a day, far from the battlefields on which they had made their sacrifice. And with bleak impassivity their last resting-place overlooks the most hated place in all of France in those years of war, the Bull Ring of Étaples.

'It was a hellish dump without a single redeeming feature,' wrote one veteran, Corporal Reynolds from Leicester.

'I can truthfully say,' wrote another soldier, 'that I had

moments there as unpleasant as any on the Western Front. I was never so angry elsewhere.'

'It was a killer, sand everywhere, dreadful,' recalled John Musgrove from Wallsend-on-Tyne.

Étaples displayed the crucifixion of the British soldier daily in a fearful triptych: the perfunctory notes of the 'Last Post' sounded like an endless loop of dismal muzak on the brow of the hill; at its foot was the parade of victims lashed by their wrists in Army Field Punishment No. 1; and in the deadening sand and silt of the beach beyond, hundreds, thousands of troops were abused and mauled by instructors whose violence and sadism were to be remembered even after some of the horrors of the battlefields themselves faded from the mind. This was the British Army's No. 1 training camp. Its régime was so sickeningly brutal that men were to plead to go up the line and face the enemy.

'I applied to get out and go to the battlefield,' wrote Private J. McCormick of the Seaforth Highlanders, who now lives in Saltcoats, Ayrshire. 'I would get more peace there.'

Private Bradfield from King's Lynn says: 'Every man who passed through the Bull Ring so hated the staff that I wouldn't have given them a cat's chance if they'd come up the line. They were bastards all of them.'

Small wonder that Étaples was to be the scene of a frantic wild uprising — an eruption that was to turn into six days of open mutiny with 100,000 men immobilized in the vital week before the start of the Passchendaele offensive, with thousands of them hunting down police and officers, and infantry and cavalry pulled out of the line to put them down. Étaples also had one unique ingredient to contribute to the poteen of rebellion: besides humiliation and degradation inside the base, there was defiance outside it.

In the woods around the base camp, in patches of firm ground among the coastal bogs, in chalk dugouts on the wild downland, was a small army of deserters. Travelling by night, hiding by day, living by 'lifting' food from farms, Percy Toplis had made his way to the coast at Étaples by early June 1917. He was there gathered into the Sanctuary, the most elaborate and bizarre underground society in all the long subterranean civilization of the Western Front. From the sand-dunes of Berck and Paris Plage, past Le Touquet and Étaples and up through the woods towards Boulogne, there had grown up, from 1915 onwards, a metropolis of the nether world, its forum in the caves and pits round Camiers, its highways the labyrinthine chalk tunnels which honeycombed the hinterland, its residences dugouts, furnished, lit, warmed to a standard that made the trenches and billets of war seem a barbarous dream.

There, tantalizingly almost within sight of England just twenty miles away across the Channel, deserters plied the trades of the underworld until the chance came to get a boat, flee to Paris or simply melt into the complaisant community of lonely Frenchwomen left behind by conscription and the war. Sporadically the British authorities attempted to flush them out. But they were men of infinite resources. One of the British secret policemen employed to try and undermine the Sanctuary recalled that among the men he caught were veterans of two or even three years in the tunnels:

'Sometimes they were armed with revolvers, but the weapons mostly favoured and carried were sand-bags, or "thuds" as they were termed. These simple but effective weapons were improvised from the white linen ration bags — their creation being simplicity itself. Just sufficient sand was placed in the bag, which was then screwed and tied up tightly. Rifle barrels, quartered and filed down conveniently for the pocket, knives, daggers, pieces of solid rubber tyres, ash entrenching-tool handles with an iron end, short sticks, knuckle-dusters, pieces of chain — many and varied were the crude weapons found on these men.

'Not only did the deserters rob civilians, but mixing with the huge general mass of troops in the vast base headquarters would take an opportunity of running crown-and-anchor boards, shooting dice, three-card manipulation and any other manoeuvre whereby they might acquire money. If not in these ways, then they would rob army hostels, canteens and officers' messes. It was impossible to stop and question every man on the roads around and in Étaples. There were colonials masquerading as English and English dressed as colonials and a large proportion of men dressed as officers in stolen uniforms.

'Gambling in those times was nothing. The Military Police were powerless. In fact the Military Police applied Nelson's tactic of the blind eye to the telescope. It was regarded as a safety valve, and so long as there was no trouble or rioting the troops could do as they liked. I have seen many times the "Top of the Hill", as it was termed, reminiscent of Epsom Downs on Derby Day, only with no conglomeration of male and female fashion, but simply of khaki and hospital blue. Tommies with Cockney, Midland, Northern, Scottish, Irish and Colonial accents all shouting the odds like bookmakers on the racecourse. You might hear such invitations as, "What about a flutter at the old mud hook," being crown and anchor. If you didn't like the status of this military bookmaker, there would be another on his left shouting out such encouragement as, "Come on, me lucky lads. You win 'em and I'll pay," or, "The old firm, the old firm." Some enterprising Tommies went so far as to get boards painted advertising their stands. To see a Tommy with an old black or grey silk top-hat or bowler, or even with a bookmaker's satchel was quite a common sight. There were crude notices painted on gutta-percha ground-sheets, "No limit. Five francs to five million. Jock of Pontius Pilate's Bodyguard. Old Digger of the Aussies. Old Darkie of the Diehards, the Sky's My Limit".'

It was in and among such an atmosphere that the absentee would move, safe in the assurance of the old saying, 'There's safety in numbers.' Among hundreds of thousands of soldiers, all odds were against his detection, provided he used caution. The place was made for that prince of masquerade, Percy Toplis. Dressed, according to mood, as a captain, a sergeant-major, or even in moments of convenient diffidence as a corporal, Toplis set about turning the confusion of Étaples base headquarters into a comfortable living. Only later was he to help to turn it into an insurrection.

The Étaples base that he entered for the second time in that third year of the war, 1917, was, however, already moving towards an explosion. Brigadier-General Thomson's olympian vision of his task as base commander had remained unruffled during a year in which his staff had refined Étaples into a unique short course in brutality and persecution.

'One PT sergeant was so maltreating the soldiers in the Bull Ring that I had a dust-up with him and laid a complaint,' recollects Company Sergeant-Major John Gray of the Gordon Highlanders, 'but I was just rapidly posted away to the front.'

The new draft, arriving at Boulogne from Folkestone, fell instantly into the clutches of the infamous 'Canaries' — the permanent instructors at the camp. They wore yellow armbands, and took less than a fortnight to earn the undying hatred of almost every man among the million or more who passed through their hands.

'They were the worst type of man imaginable,' comments Private Notley of Norwich. 'It was rumoured that some of them came from the glass-house at Aldershot. They made men's lives a misery.'

The Canaries took over the new soldiers on the twenty-mile route-march from Boulogne. This had been General Thomson's idea back in April, to start toughening the troops up straight away. 'A rest camp has been established at Neufchâtel for a midday rest,' his diary generously records. His soldiers remember it as a hut where they got half a slice of bread and the use of a cold tap. And the shouting started immediately the march was under way. Any man with a blister on his foot or any sign of flagging from the double-quick infantry pace was harried, sworn at, threatened.

'The whole approach from Boulogne was depressing,' recalls Private Notley, 'with hospitals and cemeteries lining the whole route. When we got to Étaples, it was new kit and rifles and more abuse until we got to our quarters.'

The vast array of candidates for the front line was corralled behind barbed wire into a series of infantry base depots (IBDs). These stretched on either side of a road for a mile or more up a hill behind the town of Étaples itself. Étaples, a little fishing port on the River Canche, with its classic French main square with cafés and bars, was out of bounds to the Bull Ring troops. The only means of access — bridges across the railway and the river — were held day and night by a rota of petty Horatios ordered to deflect all-comers from the perilous delights of a glass of wine at an *estaminet* or an evening at the town cinema.

Only officers and instructors were allowed across to the two brothels, or to sample the wares of La Comtesse, Étaples's most flamboyant whore, who drove ostentatiously round the main square of an evening in an open carriage and pair. Yet even this restricted jollification caused General Thomson endless worry. Throughout the spring and summer of 1917, while the base camp seethed beneath him, the commandant seemed to concentrate his thoughts mainly on the much-needed VD hospital for officers, to judge from his diary entries:

[February:] Work on venereal hospital for officers has not yet been started.
[March:] Officers' venereal hospital not started but site is pegged out.
[April:] Building for officers' venereal hospital in progress.
[May:] Work nearing completion.
[June — triumphantly:] Officers' venereal hospital opened on the 21st.

In the cauldron that was to produce the most serious threats to discipline in the entire war, no other subject got more of the commandant's attention than the venereal welfare of his officers. He made certain that other ranks were not exposed to the risk of infection by the simple expedient of keeping them locked up. But the actual bacillus

63

which was to inflame Étaples and wreck Thomson's career was being cultured, to his apparent unconcern, four miles away from the Étaples hospitals in the infamous Bull Ring. Each new arrival met it on his first morning.

Reveille at 5 a.m. Herded out of the bell-tents where they slept crammed up to twenty-two in one tent. Given breakfast and the day's rations of one slice of bread. Then formed up with full kit and rifle for the four-mile march to the beach. The Scots sometimes marched to the pipes; the New Zealanders had their own band. But none could avoid the day's opening cacophony in the corridor of insult known as the 'Canary Run'. The instructors were lined up five or six feet apart on either side of the road. Through the gauntlet of ranting, swearing Canaries, the troops passed at the quick march. Any man whose rifle was not at the correct slope, whose puttee was loose or unsymmetrical, who had any mark on a uniform, would be swamped in a torrent of oaths. The physical trials of the Bull Ring were ruthless to the point of inhumanity, but for many soldiers it is the daily concentrated gauntlet of degradation in the 'Canary Run' which lives with them most.

'Even now, in my eightieth year,' writes Private Notley, 'I remember the abuse heaped on the rank and file there and wonder what comradeship means.'

The Bull Ring itself was merely a set of staked-out patches in the sand-hills. It was tailor-made to compound the torments of the instructors. In the heat of the summer, high collars had to stay tightly buttoned, sleeves immaculately rolled down. The soft sand dragged at the ankles. Wet, it stained the khaki of the uniforms to the fury of the Canaries. Dry, it penetrated collar and cuff to rasp the flesh red against the coarse serge. The sand exacerbated everything. The soldiers dug at the soft sand. Inevitably, immediately, it trickled back and scorned their efforts. The instructors raged. The sand muffled all sound and made it impossible to keep step. The instructors savaged the defaulters. In the frightening dark of the gas chamber where the crude gas-masks were tested, there was sand to drag the

64

feet so that escape seemed as remote as in a nightmare.

Private David Paton of Dundee remembers this as the worst of all the trials of the Bull Ring. 'You thought you would collapse and choke for ever in that deep sand. If you took too long the Canaries were there to swear and send you through again.'

Always the instructors held the whip-hand.

'They were just a lot of bullies,' said Private Joe Perks of Dundee. 'Front-line dodgers, I would call them. If you answered them back you were for the high jump. The training was much worse than normal training. Say you were doing skirmishing. If it wasn't to their satisfaction they made you do it over and over again. I've seen people getting it maybe six times a day, the same thing over and over until the best-disciplined men lost their rag and lashed out. Then it would be seven days' field punishment. They had a fence at the Bull Ring, and often there would be rows of men tied to it no matter what the weather. It happened to me once. They marched you out and tied you by the wrists. You just stood there. You couldn't ease yourself. Nothing. It was like the Foreign Legion. It did cause hatred, but usually the discipline overruled that.'

At twelve o'clock there was a halt. The one slice of bread could be eaten. For a moment, a glimmer of humanity was allowed on to the beach in the form of Lady Angela Forbes's charity tea canteen, which would later attract the wrath of Haig himself. The ration was half a pint of tea per man.

'It was an odd sort of tea, you know, dishwater. But it was better than the army supplied, which was nothing. They came down with it on a trolley and you marched up and got your tankard.'

Then it was back for the afternoon session. The Bull Ring was laid out for more than a mile on either side of the Boulogne Road and furnished with specimens of every catastrophe likely to confront the soldier. He was shown down what was laughingly known as Fleet Street, with twenty-nine different types of wire and trenching device. There was a three-day-event-style course, with drop-jump, post and rails, something known as the confidence planks, and a vaulting bar. It was right beside the road, and seemed principally reserved for exhausting minor defaulters. There was a complete model battlefield with every sophistication of dugout and trench. But this also seems to have had little attention from the instructors. What they liked principally was bayonet fighting.

There were bayonet sacks in the drill area, bayonet sacks in the trench lay-out, bayonet sacks in the attack area. Hour after hour the men in full kit were made to charge with full pack and fixed bayonets, through barbed wire and into water, leaping trenches, climbing walls, downhill and uphill, running, stumbling, scrambling up again while, as one victim wrote, the Canaries chirped: 'Get a move on, blast you. Put some guts into it. Forget you're white men. Stick it in. Don't tickle him. What's the good of shoving it there? You've got to take his life not his voice. Like to have a rest, wouldn't you?'

The same soldier remembers: 'At Étaples we were treated in a manner which made us ashamed to be soldiers. It made us bitter. But, considering ourselves old campaigners, we resented still more the treatment accorded to drafts fresh from England, boys whose physical condition was not up to it: the sectional rushes, the belly-flopping, the "On the 'ands downing", the marching, the manual drill, the saluting at every few steps. What a bad war it was at Étaples.'

After the one slice of bread and tea the training would often go on until four or five in the afternoon. And so did the persecution. As the Gordon Highlander, David Stuart of Clydebank, was coming out of the Bull Ring one day 'just about all in': 'I said to my mate, thank God that day's over. Anything for an excuse with the Canaries. They called the two of us out of the parade and gave us another hour on the assault course.'

No one remembers that the Bull Ring produced anything except resentment. But the gun and bomb ranges had a fatuity which was especially ironic for the front-line veterans.

'Old hands considered it a joke to spend time playing with strange gear like the trench catapult and the West spring gun (grenades always fell off the silly arm),' is Charles Richards of Auckland's memory.

And Joe Perks says: 'They had a special line in jam-tin bombs. You filled the jam tin with stones, put your gun cotton inside with a fuse and lit it with your cigarette. It did about as much damage as a pea-shooter.'

Sporadically there were grisly incidents: a hand blown off when a nervous youth failed to throw his grenade over the target wire and it bounded back. Corporal Reynolds heard of more than one instructor 'accidentally' bayoneted on the ranges. One legendary tale recounted how a young boy blew the brains out of a Canary at point-blank range. He was supposed to be firing blanks during the practice course, and the most vicious instructor was standing in front, laying into him about his shaky aim. The youth slipped a live round into the rifle and squeezed the trigger.

The march back to camp was the final trial.

'Whatever the weather, a man or boy was expected to be as alert and smart as if the day had just started,' recalls Private Wood of Manchester. 'Again the Canaries were there, lined up, ranting away.'

Sixty years on, his bitterness is unalloyed.

'That Étaples base camp held more bloody scroungers both in officers, sergeants and men than any camp in England or France. They dodged the trenches while there were young men of eighteen years dying, being gassed, wounded, taken prisoner.'

There is no doubt that this feeling was at the heart of the eruption which was to follow in September 1917. The conscripts who came reluctantly to fill the holes in Kitchener's slaughtered volunteer army were full of resent-ment. But the mutiny could never have raged as widely and venomously as it did without the deep feeling among those who had seen Arras, Messines, the Somme that they were being humiliated and exploited by people clinging tightly to cushy lives away from the carnage of the front:

67

military police, admin. men, instructors, the whole despised gang of 'base wallahs'.

In retrospect, the notorious base camp has its bizarre, almost comic aspects. There was the messenger-dog barracks for the motley canine regiment drafted in to train for the front line, and there was the pigeon barracks. There was the WAAC quarters, guarded even more closely than the prisoner-of-war cages, and the Under-Age battalion. Here boys, often veterans of the battlefields who had been discovered or betrayed as lying about their ages, were collected and fattened up until either they reached the age of nineteen or their chest measurements matched up to War Office requirements for the fighting man.

More immediate entertainment was in short supply. There was a wood of beech trees alongside the camp with a notice in English: 'These woods have been given for the recreation of the troops by M. de Roquigny'. Lady Angela Forbes organized a bath-house and a beer-hut, but at eight o'clock it closed to all but officers. She also owned a donkey which roamed the camp and provided, at least for Private Perks and his friends, a doleful rodeo. There was the Salvation Army hut. There was the Expeditionary Force canteen, but as Charles Richards says, there was little comfort there.

'As the Aussies and Canadians got four shillings a day and Tommy Atkins only one, the canteen was invariably bought out — especially as the Aussie mess-tin could hold four pints.'

Bathing in the sea was forbidden — a small but infuriating restriction to be added to the list of the mutineers' grievances. There was a small cinema. But spare time mainly meant sitting round the long trestle tables near the mess tent, cleaning equipment and writing letters home.

One constant distraction, however, is common to all armies away from the fighting line: the charms of the fairer sex. There were the two little brothels which were causing such heartache to Brigadier-General Thomson, not to mention La Comtesse.

68

'And for any man who could beat the system, there was an *estaminet* on the rue des Hautes Communes,' says Corporal Reynolds. 'It was run by Madame Walle and her three daughters Alice, Madeline and Lycette with no hanky-panky. Supplies were very scarce, chiefly egg and chips, but they did their best at fair prices. Alice kept order, aided by a back-handed chop to the throat which would have been no discredit to Steve Vidor.'

The hundreds of nurses serving the hospitals at Le Touquet, Paris Plage and Camiers were equally if more genteelly unavailable. Nurse Dorothy Barefoot, who came from Ottawa with the No. 1 Canadian General Hospital to Étaples, spent such little time off as she had from the mutilation in the wards at the little cafés of Paris Plage.

'The most popular spot was a little place called Le Chat Bleu tucked away amid the smart shops. There was a nice little hotel in Étaples called Les Voyageurs where we sometimes had dinner. Good food and the walls covered with paintings from artists who had paid for a meal that way before the war. We went on bicycle rides through the countryside. There were occasional parties and dances in the recreation hall, but Dame Maude McCarthy, our chief, considered such things unsuitable. It was only later when the American girls arrived enthusiastic for some relaxation after the heart-breaking duties in the wards that the ban was lifted.'

Even on the wrong side of the railway tracks, in the great base camp itself, there were some carefree possibilities, but only if you knew the ropes. Private Parrott of Leeds arrived at Étaples with the 3rd London Regiment with the benefit of a brother, Sergeant Fred, long established on the base hospital staff.

'He gave me a good time, including a very welcome bath, a complete change of uniform, civilian food and wine, and last, but by no means least, a nice young WAAC whose philosophy was "Live for today, for tomorrow we may die", which approximated to my own ideas. The next day we were marshalled into the cattle-trucks again to God knows where.'

Some nice young WAACS undoubtedly risked punishment by providing a warm Godspeed to the men leaving for the front, though the history of this aspect of their war service does not find its proper place of honour in the official memoirs. Nor does the fateful relationship between a WAAC and a Gordon Highlander which was to catapult the Étaples camp into rebellion. But while it was a love story which started the Étaples mutiny, it was the presence of the Australians which made such a thing seem possible to the British Tommy. The Aussies were indeed an eye-opener for the British troops. For three years the British had not only gone unquestioning to the slaughter at the front, but had endured the harshest régime of Victorian discipline whenever they came out of the line. Field punishment awaited any man who jibbed at a superior's orders, the firing squad any man who deserted, showed cowardice or even nodded off to sleep on duty. The class system imposed a succession of increasingly callow public-school officers on even the most battle-hardened troops.

By 1917, the British were fertile ground for the talk of peace at the Stockholm Conference of the Socialist International, and even for the propaganda of revolution which seeped out of Russia. More immediately and vividly, the Aussies reminded Tommy daily that the system was neither immutable nor essential. Gallipoli, the Somme, Ypres had taught them that the Aussies fought as bravely as any man in battle. But, despite Haig's urgings, there was no death penalty in the Australian Army. The Aussie officer often came from the ranks of the fighting troops. And when the Aussie soldier went back for a rest, he stood no nonsense about military protocol. It was the Aussies who dominated the pontoon schools and the gambling at Étaples. And they felt protective towards the Scots whom they saw as innocents trapped under the harsh discipline of the English. Toplis had seen them cut down a field punishment victim earlier in 1917. By August, Private Jellie from Auckland witnessed them cut down every prisoner at the military police compound. They would never salute an officer at Étaples, or stand for any interference from the Red Caps. In July there was a fist fight when two Aussies tried to cross the bridge to go into Étaples town. Within minutes, half of Queensland joined in the brawl, until a military policeman drew his revolver and wounded one.

To the Scots in particular it was a seminar in liberation. Private Joe Perks enlisted after he had been fired from a Dundee jute factory for whistling while he worked, and was amazed to meet men who defied exploitation of any kind:

'They were the greatest gamblers in the world. I've seen the sergeant of the Military Police come along, and they'd just say, "Go on, buzz off. Don't bother us." They'd go because they couldn't do anything with them. The men were there to fight, and when there was no fighting they wanted their pleasures. That's the way it went. The Australians were the greatest blokes I ever met. I remember when I came out of hospital at Étaples after trench fever and I went to get my hair cut. The barber holds out his hand: "That will be half a franc." There was this big Australian sitting there, and he says: "You want half a franc. The bloke doesn't have half a franc. He doesn't have a Woodbine. He's just down the line. He's been up there fighting, with you lounging and scrounging about back here. No, no," he says, "if you don't behave yourself I'll give you a good hiding." John, this Australian was called. He took me down to the canteen and bought me a few cakes and fags and gave me his post office box number. He was a sheep-shearer. "Fancy him wanting half a franc top and him getting paid for it as well," he says. "No, I'm not having anything like that." '

When the mutiny came to Étaples, the combination of the Scots and the Australians, the special grievances of the New Zealanders, the oratory of Percy Toplis, the common hatred of the Red Caps and Canaries, the burgeoning populism purveyed by papers like *John Bull*, were together to prove a deadly mix. For six days Brigadier-General Thomson and his staff would stand helplessly by and watch the old order collapse and threaten the fighting ability of the British Army, just as their ally on the Eastern Front,

Russia, was about to be levered out of the war for good by revolution.

As an officer in the Manchester Regiment, the poet Wilfred Owen had written a letter to his mother in which he described Étaples:

> I lay awake in a windy tent in the middle of a vast, dreadful encampment.
>
> It seemed neither France nor England, but a kind of paddock where the beasts are kept a few days before the shambles. I heard the revelling of the Scotch troops, who are now dead, and who knew they would be dead.
>
> I thought of the very strange look on all faces in that camp; an incomprehensible look, which a man will never see in England; nor can it be seen in any battle. But only in Étaples.
>
> It was not despair, or terror, it was more terrible than terror, for it was a blindfold look, and without expression, like a dead rabbit's.

On 9 September 1917, the beasts would break out of the paddock. A complete breakdown in Anglo-American communications was to add to an already formidable list of reasons for the havoc they would wreak.

8

When the Germans dropped seven bombs on the American-run hospital for British wounded at Étaples at around 11 p.m. on the night of Tuesday, 3 Deptember, september killing one US officer and three other ranks and wounding several other Americans, the blast was felt all over the United States, uniting a deeply divided nation suffering from serious second thoughts about being in the war at all. It was a considerable psychological blunder by the Germans, who had intended the reverse effect. Reports reaching Germany in the summer of 1917 from America showed that the resolve of the United States had weakened greatly since President Wilson's declaration of war in April.

The well-organized anti-war factions throughout the US had been gaining a sympathetic audience. Loyalists were losing a serious and bitter internal struggle against what had become widely known as 'the enemy within'. The German intention was to add weight to the arguments of their supporting millions in America with a show of brutal force which would swing the pendulum further their way and perhaps influence a US withdrawal from the war, even at that late stage. Instead, the pro-war Wilsonites found themselves handed the ideal propaganda bludgeon. At last,

73

they were able to declare, Americans had experienced the 'barbarity of the Hun'.

The hospital bombing at Étaples was hailed in the United States as the end of the phoney-war period and the answer to those who had doubted the wisdom of being involved. Because of communications confusion between General Thomson and the remote American military commanders in France, news the American government so desperately wanted to hear dawdled its way across the Atlantic. The story did not break until the morning of Saturday, 8 September, when the *New York Tribune* ran this leader, headlined 'THE HUN':

The announcement that an American medical officer has been murdered and three others wounded in a German air attack upon an American hospital on the French coast will surprise American people merely because distance has so far served to supplement their faith in human nature and make it impossible for them to believe that even Germany would do the things they have been charged with doing.

Yet there is nothing new in this German attack upon a hospital far removed from the scene of operations. The truth is that this is the sort of thing the German does. He rapes women, tortures old men, murders children, burns villages, enslaves populations, attacks hospitals, because in the German mind this is a method of making war which promises profit to the German cause.

The reason why all talk of peace is futile and sometimes approaches sin is that it is impossible for men and women to live at peace with a people who do the things that Germans do. The Canadian people hesitated to believe the French and British accounts of German atrocities until Canadian soldiers reported that some of their wounded had been crucified before Ypres. The British troops hesitated to believe what French rumors told and Belgian reports asserted, with reference to German methods of making war until British soldiers

74

occupied districts in France that had been held by Germans — until they saw what Germans had done to the women and children and the old men of the districts of Artois and Flanders.

We had our first contact with the German method in the *Lusitania*. We have not yet had sufficient contact to supply American evidence to the mass of the American people. That is coming. We have thousands of American soldiers in Europe, and we shall go to every corner of the United States, and these letters from the men at the front and in touch with the German will serve to educate the people of the United States as to the kind of thing the German is in the world of today.

The British call the German a Hun. The French call him a Boche. Both names are the expression of the mingled horror and contempt of a civilized people in presence of the barbarism of a people who do the sort of thing the German does. To the Frenchman a Boche is a kind of animal who does things that the German has done in all the defenceless villages of the North of France. To the Englishman a Hun means a kind of beast who does the things that have been done in Flanders and in Artois under the eyes of the British soldiers.

We in the United States are going to know the German as he is presently. The voices which now clamor for peace with reconciliation will fall to silence when the Germans have murdered enough of our women nurses and our men physicians and tortured enough of our soldiers to create in America the kind of conviction that similar methods have created in France and in England. The difficulty in the American case has been one of bringing home to the mass of the common people far removed from Europe the plain fact of what the German was doing. To them the war remained a remote struggle between nations. It will not long remain a remote struggle now that the Germans have taken to murdering Americans, now that they have taken to making war upon our hospitals; now that they have adopted toward us the tactics of terribleness familiar

75

to all the big and little nations of Europe. It will not be long now until every American voice is raised in support of a war which strikes at this German peril.

Different versions of this powerful, heady propaganda appeared in newspapers throughout the United States. But what was sauce for the American gander was not necessarily sauce for the British goose. The German attack on the American-manned Étaples hospital, one of six for British wounded in and around the town, was being used to stiffen the US spine. The raid was beginning to boomerang on the Germans from the American viewpoint, but it was having another effect, also not intended. The raid had lowered British morale at Étaples even further, pushing an army nearer still to mutiny.

It was only a week earlier that most of the tented hospital had been blown down by a wild storm, putting 2,831 beds out of action. The rain-soaked wounded suffered badly, and many had died as a result. And now it was necessary to endure bombing. Several British wounded had also been further injured in the air-raid, but no fuss was being made about that. After all, British troops had been dying daily for years in those hospitals. It was hardly news.

But the first American casualties of the war did make news — big news. General Thomson's official record for 2 September at Étaples reads simply: 'Enemy Aeroplane Raid. Seven bombs dropped in hospital area. Lieutenant W. T. Fitzsimmons U.S.A. and three other rank Americans killed.' This meagre record of a very important moment in history reflected how the significance of the event was lost on Thomson.

The British Command's attempts to convey the news to the American Command were likewise leisurely in the extreme, and handicapped by a lack of exact knowledge as to where that command could be located. The American General Officer Commanding, Major General John J. Pershing, after landing with a token force of several hundred at Saint-Nazaire on 26 June, had set up his

76

headquarters in an unexpected and scarcely strategic spot, Paris. Not that his presence nearer the front would have made much difference.

America had been so unprepared for war that even the token force she had sent lacked the necessary equipment to take any active part in the fighting. Pershing had made a public speech predicting that America would not be able to have a fighting force at the front before 1918, and was acting accordingly. In this first week of September he was not at the Paris hotel address where he was usually to be found. A hint from the Secretary of State for War, Newton D. Baker, that the French capital was perhaps not the best place from which to conduct the US war effort, meant that he was in the process of shifting his headquarters to the Damremont Barracks at Chaumont behind the Lorraine Front.

Thomson solved his problem by sending a dispatch to the military attaché at the US Embassy in London, where it did not arrive until the 7th. The names of dead other ranks did not rate a mention in Thomson's book, so there was more confusion which led to the *New York Tribune* and the American press generally reporting at first that only Lieutenant Fitzsimmons had been killed, with others wounded. The *New York Herald* made the most of what it had been given. Its Saturday issue had a seven-column, page 1, headline: 'Prussians murder and maim Americans in Air Attack on Hospital in France.' The story went on to state that the Prussians had 'set a new mark for frightfulness by deliberate attempts to destroy institutions of mercy'.

Other newspapers also presented the story in a manner calculated to whip up a much-needed, long-overdue public frenzy. The word 'murder' was freely used, and the more quaint 'frightfulness' much exercised. But then a frightful thing did happen to the *Herald* itself. On 13 September it wrongly corrected a second agency dispatch it had carried on the 11th stating that Fitzsimmons and three others had died. This second piece of confusion was caused by the US War Department belatedly getting to grips with events at

77

Étaples and issuing a statement giving the names of nine wounded men and nurses in addition to the four dead already reported by the military attaché in London. The *Herald* understood this statement to be instead of the first, and to mean that no one had been killed after all. It ran a single-column story to this effect on page 11. Undaunted, however, the *Herald* did find its first dead war hero in the same issue, and a curious story it was, culminating in the first bugles blowing at a military funeral in the heart of the Bronx. The *Herald*'s exclusive read:

Private Flynn, of New York, First to Die at Yaphank.
One-Time Fireman, Physically Perfect, Victim of Acute Indigestion.
(Special Despatch to the Herald.)
Camp Upton, Yaphank, L.I.

Friday: Private Harry E. Flynn, a fireman of hook and ladder truck No. 7 New York City, until he was selected for the National Army, died last night, the first selected man to die in Camp Upton. He had been ill only a few hours, of acute indigestion.

Military honours will be paid to Flynn when his body is sent to New York tomorrow.

What the *Herald* did not give was the background to Private Flynn's short and undistinguished military career in the Long Island camp fifteen miles from his home. He had never actually worn a uniform because there were no uniforms available. He had paraded and route-marched in his own shoes because there were no army boots. And he had trained and drilled with a broomstick because there were no rifles. Almost the entire US Army was without rifles, but Baker, the War Secretary, had promised them some by Christmas.

When the bugles stopped blowing at 204 Morris Avenue, the Bronx, that Sunday, the Stars and Stripes was lifted from Harry Flynn's coffin and — as the US military manual stipulates — presented to his next-of-kin, Uncle Tom, as a symbol of the fact that the deceased had served in the Armed Forces of the United States, and that his country, in conducting part one of his ceremonial interment, had given its final and solemn recognition of the obligation which it owed to a faithful servant. One of America's first dead war heroes deserved the tribute no less because he had seemingly died of indigestion while briefly serving in the Unarmed Forces of the United States.

Other newspapers continued to devote columns of space to the first American war dead in the week following the announcement of the 'Étaples horror'. The *Christian Science Monitor* revealed that General Pershing had been rebuked by the War Department for being slow off the mark at Étaples. He had been instructed to put casualties at the start of his daily cable message in future. He responded to the call to emphasize the human cost of American participation in the war with a first casualty list showing that Sergeant M. G. Calderwood and Private W. F. Brannigan had been slightly wounded by shell fragments. Engineers Brannigan and Calderwood had been repairing a railway line, and the US press speculated about how close to the front line they had actually been. The *New York Times* carried one sentence showing British casualties, dead and seriously wounded, during August: 58,811.

The Étaples dead, First Lieutenant William Fitzsimmons (28), a doctor from Kansas City, and the three medical orderlies Privates Leslie Woods (17), of Streaton, Illinois, Rudolph Rubino (20), of New York, and Oscar Tugo (22), of Boston, had all volunteered for service attached to the Red Cross before the United States entered the war. Obituaries continued to be written about them at great length. Their families were interviewed for quotes about how proud they felt, and at Étaples on 7 September a seven-strong American press corps invaded the area to the great disgust of the British troops, whose wounded were ignored. The reporters sent back stories that the German pilot had not only unleashed bombs. He had showered the ground

79

with German pfennigs, thereby showing Prussian contempt for American capitalism and proving that the Germans had deliberately singled out a hospital where they knew there would be US personnel.

The British soldiers were further soured the following day when General Thomson instructed a British colonel to show the American journalists round the Bull Ring itself, as though it were some showpiece of British militarism. The truth was that the hospitals should never have been sited close to railway stations like that at Étaples, which were, of course, legitimate bombing targets for the enemy. Day and night the trains conveyed men and guns to the front. Yet four of the hospitals were in a cluster directly alongside the tracks. Indeed, as the soldiers knew, this placing of the hospitals was in direct breach of an international Red Cross agreement.

A true understanding of the great pandemonium created by the raid could only have been gained by a study of America's uneasy position on her home front at the time. The truth was that the US looked upon the German bombs as a great blessing. On the one side were anarchists and pacifists, lined up against loyalists and patriots on the other. On 9 September, when the British Army revolted at Étaples, three anarchists were shot dead by police in Milwaukee when they tried to break up a patriotic meeting in the Italian section of the town. Two detectives were wounded. This type of clash occurred frequently.

Every main American city had at least one German-language newspaper catering for the country's huge German population. They turned out virulent anti-war propaganda, condemning US entry as capitalistic interference which did not have the support of the people. The *Elore*, a Hungarian newspaper published in New York, was trumpeting that American capitalistic interests were preparing to sacrifice the life and blood of their people and would go on doing so until the lust for booty was satisfied. All these newspapers were free to publish what they liked.

There were many telling incidents. In Ohio, a troop-train

travelling to an eastern port was fired upon by unknown rebels who wounded three soldiers. The Federal Department of Justice announced its intention of investigating the case of Major William Thomson of New York, who had been making anti-war speeches. The New York Master Bakers at their annual convention on 12 September passed a resolution that they were willing to make bread without profit for the duration of the war. As their president, Maximilian Strasser, explained, no baker would actually do that, but the resolution did express patriotism and the convention would get a big patriotic write-up from the newspapers. And as a demonstration of true patriotism in the face of the massive build-up of anti-war feeling through the country, the former President, Theodore Roosevelt, made a serious offer to President Wilson to personally lead a group of volunteers to fight in France. He was furious to have his offer turned down.

By the end of September the position had clarified. Legislation was being passed to control the content of foreign newspapers. Police and US marshals were rounding up aliens and spies by the thousand. America had turned Étaples to advantage. The air-raid had sparked off a mood of loyalist support which was to put 'the enemy within' on the run.

At Étaples itself it had further helped to put the British soldiers in a mood for mutiny.

81

9

There was never a real day of rest at Étaples, but Sunday was the nearest thing. Reveille sounded at 7 a.m. rather than 5 a.m. Parades and training were restricted to five periods before noon. It was also the one day when the camp cinema was open in the afternoon. Otherwise it was business as usual. Inside the huge base, the long, ugly finger of the camp incinerator belched forth its thick black smoke, dowsing the huts and tents with an ever-pervading smell of burning flesh. For along with the waste, it took the amputated limbs from the hospitals.

Alongside the railway line from Boulogne the bugles were still incessantly blowing the 'Last Post' as the dead were trundled on Union Jack-draped handcarts along to the cemetery. And at the station, with its five flower-decked platforms, the trains still hooted and steamed their way to and from the front, a hundred or more a day, even on Sundays. Those rattling their way east with human reinforcements, supplies and heavy guns passed the military cattle-trucks travelling west with their cargoes of wounded and dying.

One man who was to play a crucial role on that black day of Sunday, 9 September 1917, had planned to sleep in late.

Second-Lieutenant James Davies, Royal Fusiliers, had already faced a personal crisis that week and was being posted back to the front. He was an actor who had left the stage of the London Palladium to join the army in the first week of the war in August 1914. At the battle of Loos in September 1915 he had been a corporal with a section of the 24th Division, one of 300 survivors out of 1,100 men. He had already been wounded three times, and his grateful commanders had rewarded him with a posting to Étaples to recover. Then, on 7 September 1917, the young officer had staged his own one-man mutiny — and got away with it. It had happened when a young lieutenant had taken him to the Bull Ring to teach him how to fire a Verey pistol:

'This stupid man, whose feet looked as if they had been flattened by walking around on the sand, staged his Verey light demonstration for me and a group of fellow officers. I do not think he had been nearer the front than Étaples, and I remember thinking at the time, This surely must be the bloody end.

'It was very hot, and standing around on parade with the sun beating down on my tin hat I felt very dizzy and just sat down, to the astonishment of those around me. I felt I could not go on, but before the shouting started I ran from the Bull Ring to the adjutant's office.

'I burst in on him, shouting, "This nonsense is not making me fit to go back to my battalion. It is making me unfit. I am not going back to the Bull Ring any more." '

Davies then threw down a challenge.

'Send me back to my unit or put me under arrest.' I remember him looking up at me with some astonishment from his desk. My outburst amounted to a refusal to obey orders and, in a way, it was a mutinous stance, but with this difference. I was stating a preference, and I suppose the system had won in a way. There were many who felt the system had been ruthlessly designed to make men glad to leave Étaples for battle.

'Of course, there was this other difference. The other ranks would never have been allowed to forcibly express their desires. I was. I never went back to the Bull Ring again.'

On that last day before returning to the front, Davies had washed and shaved by 11 a.m. and joined two other officers walking into Étaples town to take the single-decker tram which ran by the side of the road to Paris Plage. They had a lunch-time drink in the Hôtel des Anglais, part of which was in use as a war hospital, followed by a leisurely stroll to the beach for an afternoon in the sun.

As the young veterans chatted desultorily about Davies's good fortune in escaping Étaples, Corporal Wood of the Gordon Highlanders, not so lucky in the fate awaiting him, strolled out of the barbed-wire compound where the Scots were billeted and down towards the cinema. Since midday it seemed to have been getting hotter and hotter, and the tantalizing glimpse of the sea below did nothing to cool the atmosphere. The Gordons had had as hellish a war as any, and Corporal Wood had seen his share. He was a popular, admired NCO. The quarantine régime in Étaples was not much of a reward.

Coming up the road towards him that afternoon, however, was one of Étaples's more welcome sights: a girl in the uniform of the WAACs, a girl he knew, from Aberdeen. Whether it was chance, a lover's tryst or a fleeting wartime assignation, this simple boy-meets-girl incident was to put the match to the tinder. Wood stopped. The two stood talking. In the heat of the afternoon the soldier lounged, his tunic unbuttoned.

They were interrupted by a military policeman. Wood recognized him as a well-known boxing champion, Private Harry Reeve. Unlike most boxers, Reeve was renowned for throwing his weight about outside as well as inside the ring. He ordered Wood to move on. Talking to WAACs wasn't allowed. In any case, the corporal was improperly dressed. There was the sudden flare of violence as the two men shouted. There was shoving and pushing, a punch was thrown. Private Reeve took out his revolver and shot Wood. Quickly the news filtered round the Scots regiments. It came for them as the final straw. The Étaples mutiny was on.

It was after eight o'clock before Davies said his good nights to the other officers, after dinner in the hotel in the Paris Plage, his intention being to walk back to base on his own. Darkness was beginning to shroud the poplar trees on the coast road, and in the shadows under the trees, Davies spotted a horse-drawn fiacre with an elderly driver. He changed his mind about walking, handed over five francs and started out over the cobbles on his journey into history.

About a quarter of a mile out from Étaples town centre the horse pricked up its ears. Davies's first reaction to the noise of distant uproar was, like that of many others that night, to think that the Germans had broken through and captured the town. He dismissed the notion. But as they drew nearer to the Town Hall end of the town centre, the din had grown deafening. They turned into the square and the horse stopped in its tracks. Davies jumped down from the fiacre.

'It was the most astonishing sight. Hundreds of troops were yelling, jeering, cheering, singing and dancing.' Davies turned and headed for his depot via the narrow iron railway bridge which was to figure so vividly in the events to follow. As he crossed the bridge he looked down on another astounding gathering. Below him several hundred troops were running amok. Tents, huts and latrines were being set on fire. By the light of the flames, the troops who had either not attempted or who had failed to break out of camp could be seen standing to in the separate compounds of their IBDs. Armed officers had chosen this method of keeping them away from the main body of mutineers. Other senior officers were rushing about, with the rioters on the outside of the parade grounds jeering at their confusion.

Davies got to his depot's wooden office in the centre of a cluster of bell-tents, some of which were ablaze. Troops were dancing around them, whooping it up like Red Indians on the warpath. A lieutenant-colonel dashed in behind him. The colonel gave his order to the adjutant, and the adjutant, as Davies puts it, 'not liking me very much', passed it on to Davies. He was to go back to the bridge in command of fifty men with fixed bayonets. And he was to stop, by force if necessary, any more rebels crashing into Étaples.

Because of the recent night air-raid on the American hospital, camp and road lighting had been restricted, but by now the lights were fully on. Searchlights had also been rushed to the scene, and as Davies marched at the head of his men their bayonets glistened and gleamed when caught in the cross-beams of light. Mutineers fell back on either side of the column, still booing, jeering and cat-calling, uncertain about their next move. When the fixed bayonets mounted the steps and took up position in two ranks across the bridge, their minds were made up.

The road into the town was being barred, so the bridge had to be taken. The rioters started moving menacingly towards the bridge with its wooden steps and iron frame-work. Davies had been plunged into a desperate situation without warning. Having lined up his soldiers behind him, he turned to face the foe, many of them friends of the rifle and bayonet holders behind his back. If he ordered them to fight off the mutineers, would they do so? And if they did obey, how much common blood would be spilled? At his back was the forbidden territory of Étaples town.

He looked down about twenty feet upon the sea of angry faces beginning to press round the bottom of the stairway. These men, his comrades in battle, had had their bravery snubbed, their patience tested beyond all endurance. Suddenly, ridiculously, says Davies, some lines from his last London Palladium part came back to him. They were, 'Gather round my braves, gather round. For I, Black Eagle, your chief, have something to say to you.'

'For one wild moment I had the idea that the tension might be broken and a bond created if I addressed the mutineers on similar lines,' he remembers ruefully.

Thunderous cheers and chants from below jolted him back to an acute awareness of his plight. The cheering signalled the first advance up the steps towards the rebels. They were coming at him, cautiously as yet, but determinedly,

86

and most frightening of all, wordlessly. Even the cheers from those inciting from behind had died. In front, in almost equal numbers, were Australians, New Zealanders and Scots. The Royal Fusiliers to his rear started to cough and uneasily shuffle their feet, but Davies continued to stand his ground without flinching.

The lemon-squeezer New Zealand hats, the wide-brimmed, side-turned-up Australian headgear, the bottle-green glengarries of the Gordon Highlanders formed the bobbing advance of a force which threatened to engulf the guardians of the bridge over Étaples railway. Somewhere to the rear of the rebels a lone piper started to play 'Highland Laddie', the regimental tune of the Gordons. The Jocks started to chorus their own adaptation of words to the music, softly at first, then more loudly, 'Bonny Wullie's gone awa, will he no come back again?'

Second-Lieutenant Davies knew the Gordons' regimental motto, 'Strike Sure', and he had seen them in reckless action in the past. He tried hard to detect if hand-guns were being carried by the rebels, but they were jammed so tightly together that he could not be certain. He had never raised his own pistol throughout, carefully keeping it dangling nonchalantly in his right hand, pointing down towards the top step immediately below where he stood.

Suddenly the piper stopped playing, the singing ceased and the threats, the cheering and the jeering drained away. They were inches apart now: a big burly Highland trooper, full of hatred born of intense grievance, leading his excitable followers in a just cause, and an understanding English officer with his finger on the trigger. Davies remembers:

'The Scotsman was so tall that though he was on the next to top step of the bridge, it had become an eyeball-to-eyeball confrontation, with me on the top step.'

Then Davies had another wildly irrelevant thought. It was that they were both improperly dressed. The wild-eyed Jock did not have his uniform collar fastened at the front, and Davies should have had a sword in his hand instead of the revolver. He broke the silence as calmly as he could. 'I don't know what the hell's been going on here today, but be a good fellow and take your crowd back to the camp. It can all be sorted out tomorrow when we've all simmered down.'

Davies had spoken evenly but loudly enough for those jamming the stairs behind the Scot to hear. They heaved closer behind their leader, trying to jostle him past Davies with shouts of, 'Tell him about the murder ... tell him we want to get the bastard police that did it.'

The leading Scotsman braced himself backwards against the crowd pushing him from behind, held up his right hand and yelled at Davies, 'Ye hear what they say, sir. It's no you we're out tae git. We've got naething against you, but I mist ask ye tae stand aside.' There was a pause. Then, in an even louder voice, the Jock added, 'And if ye don't we'll turn the machine-guns on ye.'

At this there was further rustle of uneasy movement among the soldiers behind Davies, while wild pandemonium broke out again among those before and below him. Above the general din he heard shouts of, 'Get the guns.' Davies knew there was an armoury near at hand. This highly dangerous game of poker had to end.

He turned to face his heavily outnumbered troops and ordered them to stand aside. He could see the relief flooding back into their faces. Then the fusiliers were brushed aside as the mutineers stormed past them over the bridge towards Étaples. The mutiny of Étaples was to be bloody, but it would have been bloodier still but for the brave and difficult decision by a twenty-year-old lieutenant to concede defeat. His mature example was to be followed by junior officers throughout the mutiny, to the fury of Commandant Thomson.

Davies watched the victorious mutineers surge across the bridge and down the steps at the other side, screaming and yelling in the manner he had so often seen them adopt when charging the enemy lines at the front. At the centre of the rushing, shoving, pushing phalanx was the piper, marching stolidly and imperturbably, refusing to be jostled out of tune.

Davies marched his fifty fusiliers back behind the barbed wire of their own compound where an impatient, irritated adjutant listened to explanations and decided to change tactics. At this point it was thought that not many of the rebels were armed. So the adjutant moved to confiscate as many rifles as he could.

'All arms they could get hold of were piled on the parade-ground under guard,' said Corporal Frank Edwards of the Loyal North Lancashire Regiment. 'It fell to my lot to be detailed with the picket to hold the bridge which carried the little tram-cars for Paris Plage over the River Canche. We were put in the charge of an elderly major and were formed into three groups, one at each end of the bridge, the other in the centre. I was in the second rank of the squad holding the town end of the bridge. After about twenty minutes we heard the sound of singing, and a mob of soldiers in various stages of undress swarmed into view. They were led by a Canadian private who, with his tunic unbuttoned and his cap on the back of his head, occasionally gave vent to his feelings by shouting, 'Down with the Red Caps, let's release the prisoners,' which were loudly echoed by his companions. They seemed to be attracted by our little force, and came towards us, laughing and jeering. Our commander ordered us to load, but only one man near me did so. The Canadian advanced right up to our front rank, closely followed by the mob, and the whole crowd surged forward right across the bridge. A tram-car was following closely, and the leader, together with many of his followers, boarded it. The only man to suffer being he who foolishly loaded his rifle, who had his hat thrown into the river by one of the crowd who had seen him do it.'

The adjutant decided on one last attempt. Forty officers were marched through a gauntlet of boos, jeers and catcalls to man the bridge. This time there were no preliminaries, just tough, bitter hand-to-hand fighting as lieutenants and captains grappled and wrestled with privates. As the men rushed at them up the steps, heads down, the advantage was heavily with the officers. From their superior strategic

89

position it was relatively easy to repel the onslaught by throwing or butting the attackers back down the stairs. But some did make it to the top, where the mauling became fast, furious and ferocious. Soldiers, taught by the Canaries how to handle themselves in the event of being disarmed, were handing out to their officers the benefit of their tuition.

A call had gone out from the aptly named reinforcement camp headquarters to the officers' club behind the Town Hall: 'All officers to the bridge.' Thirty more officers who had until then deemed it wise to stay away from the rioters in the square outside, ran out of a side-exit, heading for the railway. They arrived just in time to add their weight and prevent the men breaking through. And weight it was. Until then it had been an unceremonious fracas. Now it became vicious. Hitherto men had been hurled back down the steps. But their persistence had destroyed all patience. Two were hurled through the air, over the side of the bridge to the track below, and although injured, managed to crawl off the track out of the way of a trainload of troops slowly gathering speed for the Western Front. For those thus in transit it could not have been the most uplifting spectacle. Oddly enough, they cheered themselves hoarse and shouted encouragement from below before a cloud of billowing steam and smoke obscured the contest.

The men had retreated, but it was the only small victory the authorities had that night, or for another five days. And the next confrontations were to be far more ruthless and bloody. The mutineers had targets they were absolutely determined to destroy: the Red Caps and Canaries of Étaples.

About 1,500 mutineers had succeeded in making it over the railway into the town, leaving a trail of havoc and devastation. When the troops roared in, the French customers in the cafés and *estaminets* had fled to their homes, and the restaurant owners had closed their doors only to have them smashed down by the invaders.

Those who could not crash their way into the cafés because of the crowds already jammed inside had barrels of beer and wine rolled out to them in the square. Street stall-holders whose business it was to turn out soggy potato chips on paraffin-heated braziers had disappeared along with the entire local population. Behind locked doors they listened in terror to the bedlam in the square.

A mixture of threats and pleas by equally terrified military policemen and Bull Ring instructors had resulted in some of these fugitives being given refuge by householders in streets just off the square. Inside, they huddled in little groups too scared to speak as the rebels rampaged long into the night. In the rue Saint-Pierre the door of one house was smashed down by Australians and Scots who found a military policeman and a Canary hiding under the same bed. Outside the bedroom door, an elderly French fisher-man and his wife, dressed in their customary all-black Sunday-night clothes, stood weeping as the fugitives were kicked and battered and left for dead.

When the potato supply ran out back in the square, the braziers were overturned and the paraffin used to set fire to the barrels that had been drained. To these bonfires were added piles of chairs and tables taken from both inside and outside the cafés. The centre of Étaples was a wreck by the time the first officers' patrols could get there at about 11 p.m.

Many of the soldiers had started to straggle back to camp. But the main body of the mutineers had left the town and crossed the bridge over the Canche River, heading for the woods of Le Touquet and Paris Plage. The widespread rumour in the town was that the British troops were behaving in this wanton fashion because they had suffered a heavy defeat and were in retreat from the front, pursued by victorious Germans.

Sergeant Fred Parrott, RAMC, of Steep Hill, Streatham, London, was in charge of the reception room in the hospital where Corporal Wood, the first casualty of the uprising, died on the Sunday night. He remembers the

91

rumour which swept through the hospitals and the outskirts of the camp about the reported German breakthrough.

'As far as my hospital was concerned it started when two breathless nurses rushed back from the town saying that there had been a lot of noise and shooting and the local French people had told them the Germans had got through. Everybody was confined to the hospital for the rest of the day and night.'

When the truth became known, he and a medical corporal armed themselves with revolvers, dug a large hole in the sand near the hospital and hid in it, waiting to ambush any mutineers who strayed their way.

'But,' says Parrott, 'the dissidents did not get as far as us although we could hear a lot of shooting going on in the distance.'

The excitement of a very bloody Sunday died down towards midnight. But the respite was to be brief. The limited, laconic, official version of these five tumultuous days, signed by General Thomson in the War Diary, gives little away, though he must have seen the first troubles as the soldiers spilled out of the cinema across from his office window. But it does admit to another incident which stirred the cauldron that boiling Sunday afternoon. The New Zealanders, furious at stories that the British were blocking their leave, had also broken out. As the general's War Diary for the day reads:

Disturbance in Reinforcement Camp between Military Police and Troops about 6.30 p.m., Corporal Wood, 4th Gordons being accidentally shot.

About noon a Corporal from 27 Infantry Battalion Division, warned the Military Police that the New Zealanders intended raiding the Police Hut on account of a New Zealand Corporal who had been arrested by the police sometime previously. As threats by Colonials were fairly common, no notice was taken.

About 3.00 p.m. the police arrested No. 25/548 Gunner A. J. Healy, New Zealand Artillery, at Three Arch Bridge,

Étaples. Gunner Healy alleges he was arrested without any provocation and after having been assaulted by the Police.

The Corporal in charge released Gunner Healy.

The incident of the arrest of Gunner Healy was witnessed by other men, and some feeling was shown against the Police. A crowd began to gather by 4.00 p.m. and by 5.00 p.m. this crowd had increased, largely being augmented by men leaving the afternoon performance of the Cinema. About 5.30 p.m. a New Zealander went to the Police Guard Room and demanded the release of Gunner Healy. This New Zealander was shown, by being taken into the Guard Room, that the prisoner had been released. The attitude of the crowd was very threatening, stones were thrown, and attempts made to rush the Police Hut.

It was no coincidence that the New Zealanders were in the forefront of the trouble. For some days the newspapers reaching the camp had been carrying stories that the British government was resisting plans to give up to six months' leave to New Zealanders who had served in France for three years. A fortnight before, on 28 August, the Secretary of State for War, Lord Derby, had startled his fellow members in the War Cabinet by circulating among them a telegram received from New Zealand. Coming from the Governor-General of New Zealand, the Earl of Liverpool, it read:

An arrangement has been agreed to by my Government whereby after 3 years service members of the New Zealand Expeditionary Force may return on leave to Dominion; numbers to be limited to 250 per month and leave to be reckoned as 6 months from departure from the front until return which would allow 2 months in New Zealand. Detailed arrangements are being made direct with General Officer Commanding New Zealand Expeditionary Force and my Government trust that Imperial authorities will raise no objection to these arrangements.

93

This last sentence virtually defied the Cabinet not to acquiesce, a challenge immediately taken up by the War Secretary, who rushed to find an ally in the person of the Adjutant-General, Lieutenant-General Sir G.F.N. Nacready. This hastily arranged consultation enabled Lord Derby to write on 7 September, two days before the mutiny:

I circulate to the War Cabinet for their consideration a notice by the Adjutant-General on the foregoing telegram which, in his view, indicates a very dangerous line of policy.

His observations are:

If leave on this scale is to be given to the New Zealanders, irrespective of the military situation at the front, the same measure must be meted out to all troops, Dominion or British, and the result will be that the forces at the front will be completely depleted. If the privilege is confined to Dominion troops a spirit of strong antagonism which will, in my opinion, result in bloodshed, will spring up between the British and Dominion troops, between whom already, on account of the difference of pay, and the absence of the death penalty in the Australian Contingent, the feeling is not too friendly.

The first inkling of this news had reached France in the first week of September. Another element had thus been added to the flammable mixture swirling around Étaples as the great Passchendaele battle began.

In the months leading up to September there had been an increase in the number of occasions when Canaries and military policemen had been found mysteriously shot or bayoneted to death. Cause of death in these isolated but nevertheless numerous incidents had always been officially listed as 'accidental'. By September, too, many men had already been to the front once and were enduring Étaples for the second and, in some cases, the third time, having just recovered from wounds. News of Bolsheviks in Russia and mutiny in France, and deserters from the chalk pits mixing freely with the soldiers, also helped to stoke the fire. The fact that the uprising did not happen earlier was, however, only because of the transit-camp nature of Étaples. Men rarely had to put up with it for periods longer than seven to ten days before having to face what they regarded as the lesser hell, the front line. Opportunities to get together, to conspire, were few.

From the moment of the assault on the police hut, Commandant Thomson's account parts company with that of every other witness. Predictably, it tries to minimize the troubles. Even so, it must have made horrendous reading at Field-Marshal Haig's headquarters as his staff struggled to get enough reinforcements through to feed the Passchendaele offensive. Back at Folkestone, urgently needed troops were marooned waiting for the Étaples mutiny to be resolved. There was no chance of them being shipped across and into the maelstrom of a base in the grip of rebellion. Before jump-off day, ten days later, not only would reinforcements have almost come to a halt, but Haig would be bleeding the line of assault troops to put down the mutiny at his base.

Brigadier Thomson's diary for the first night of the mutiny continues:

Shots were fired from a revolver, two or three, by No. 204122 Pte. H. Reeve, Camp Police. Pte. Reeve states he had no revolver, but that a man (Australian or New Zealander) in the crowd had one which he, Pte. Reeve, snatched and fired over the heads of the crowd. The revolver was snatched from Pte. Reeve.

One man, No. 240120 Corporal W. B. Wood 4th Gordons, on the outskirts of the crowd, was hit in the head and died after admission to No. 24 General Hospital, at 8.5 p.m. same day. A French woman standing in the Rue de Heguet was also hit by a bullet. The crowd at this time, shortly after 6.00 p.m. in the vicinity of Three Arch Bridge and the Police Hut was 3,000 — 4,000 strong.

Captain V. C. Guinness, Camp Adjutant, saw the crowd at 6.15 p.m. and was then told of the shooting by the Police. He at once reported to Colonel Nason, O.C. Reinforcements, who immediately ordered a picquet of one officer, 50 other ranks from New Zealand depot. This picquet at once turned out with rifles and bayonets, but no ammunition. Colonel Nason went to the Police Hut and seeing the serious state of affairs, ordered two further picquets, each of 100 other ranks with officers from No. 19 and No. 25 IBDs. A further picquet of 1 officer, 15 other ranks was also detailed from No. 18 IBD.

At the Officers' Club, Colonel Nason ordered all officers to immediately rejoin their Depots, and each depot was ordered to send three officers to No. 2 Bridge to persuade the crowd to return.

Feeling in the crowd was only against the Police and Officers were treated respectfully. The officers gradually got the men back to camp and by 9.45-10.00 p.m. all was quiet.

During the fracas at Three Arch Bridge, and directly the shots had been fired, the demeanour of the crowd was so threatening towards the Police, that the Police disappeared.

A crowd of about 1,000 gathered in Étaples town, and about 7.30 p.m. tried to break into the Sévigné Café where two policemen were hiding. Several officers held back the crowd and the town was clear by 9.00 p.m.

Lieutenant Davies does not feel that the treatment accorded to him and other officers on the railway bridge that night was of the most 'respectful' nature. He recalls that the last salute he got was when he stepped down from the carriage which brought him back from Paris Plage. Certainly Étaples was anything but quiet by 9 p.m. And the camp was in uproar all night.

The veterans are united in disagreeing with Thomson's account of the shooting of William Wood by Harry Reeve, a pre-war welterweight boxing champion, later sentenced by court martial to one year's hard labour for manslaughter. All of them swear that the real reason for the deliberate

1 Brigadier-General Andrew Graham Thomson

2 Brigadier-General Thomson poses with junior officers and their
wives at Warminster Barracks

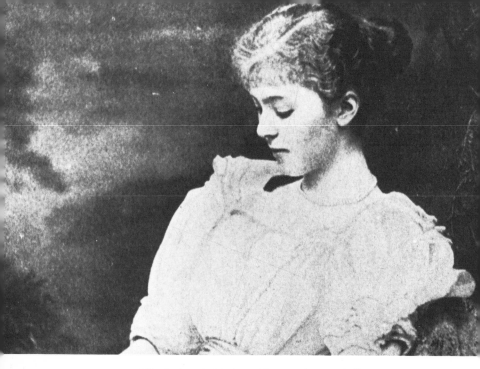

3 Lady Angela Forbes at her coming out ball
4 Lady Angela Forbes at the time of the mutiny

5 Edwin Woodhall, secret service agent

6 'Young Chips' Thomson (far right) on a family picnic in
Scotland

7 Troops at bayonet practice on the snow covered sand of the
Bull Ring

8 Lieutenant James Davies today

9 Lieutenant James Davies during the Second World War – the British Army's only one-legged infantryman

10 Corporal Frank Reynolds: a photograph taken during the First
World War

11 Corporal Frank Reynolds today

12 The burial of Corporal William Wood, whose death at the hands of a military policeman was one of the causes of the mutiny

13 WAACs tending the graves of the Étaples dead, September 1917

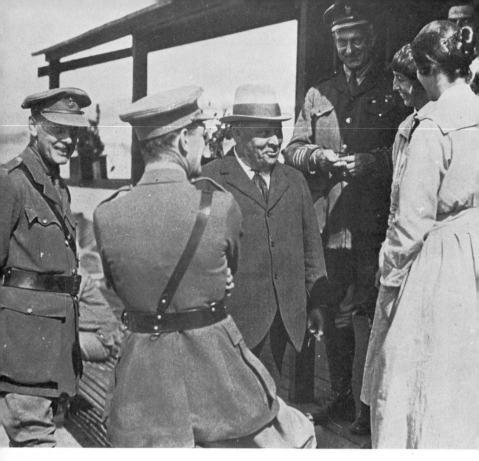

14 Horatio Bottomley, photographed at Étaples during the mutiny

15 Three Arch Bridge, around which the rebellion raged after the first day

16 The damage caused by German aerial attack on one of the Étaples hospitals

17 One of the prizes of the mutiny: a café for the troops

18 Part of the Étaples base camp

19 Norman de Courcy Parry, as he was on the night of Sunday,
6 June 1920

20 Norman de Courcy Parry today

21 A greetings card sent by Toplis from France to his mother

22 Mrs Toplis leaving Penrith in her invalid chair after the
inquest on her son

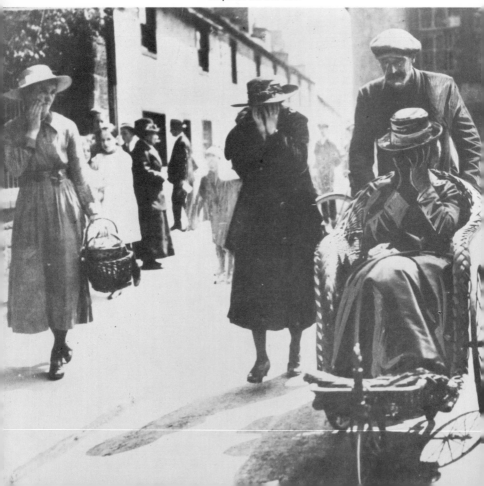

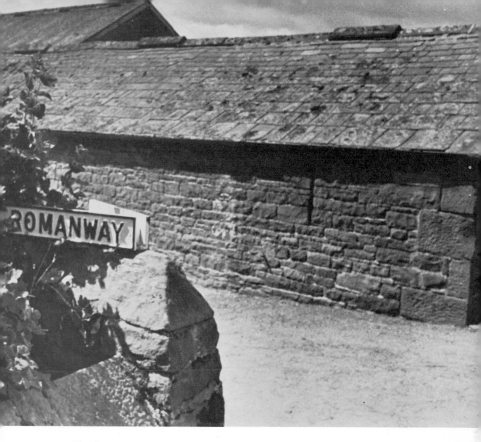

23 The farm wall behind which the police gunmen hid as they waited
for Toplis

24 The road-side memorial to Constable Fulton's uncle at the point where Toplis was to die thirty-five years later

25   Author William Allison at the place of Toplis's secret burial

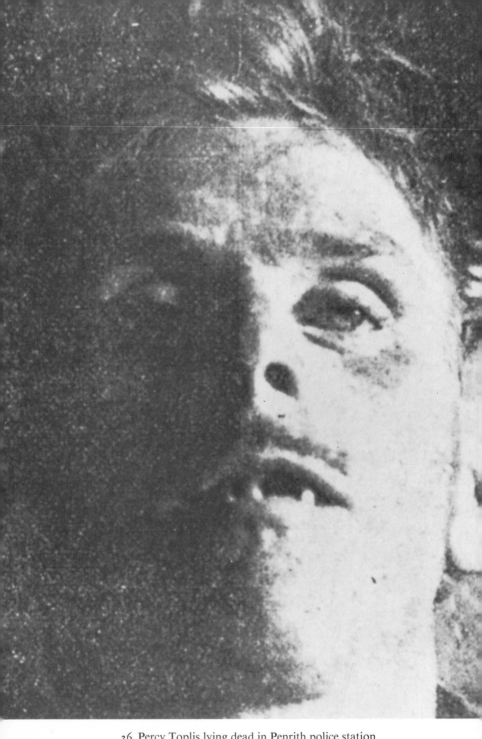

26 Percy Toplis lying dead in Penrith police station

shooting of Wood was that Reeve caught him speaking to the WAAC.

Thomas McNab (86), Royal Flying Corps, of 352 Main Street, Glasgow, witnessed the last part of that drama outside the cinema: 'This military policeman was being dragged along the ground by two soldiers. A crowd of soldiers followed on taking it in turns to hit him and kick him. I saw an Aussie belting the captured policeman with a long stick. The policeman was howling out in agony.'

Indeed memories are vivid, and, after sixty years, remarkably unanimous about that night and the extraordinary days that followed. And the men who remember were not riff-raff or draft-dodgers, but often among the bravest who had seen action since the earliest days of the war.

Frank Reynolds (82) of 5 Stoughton Drive, Evington, Leicester, ran a chemist's business until he retired at the age of 72. He was a founder member of the Old Comrades Association before it became the British Legion, of which he is a vice-president. In September 1917 he was a corporal in the 2nd Suffolk Regiment and already held the Military Medal for bravery at the Somme in 1916, where he received wounds which subsequently resulted in the loss of an eye.

In that first explosion of anger, Reynolds helped to launch an attack on General Thomson's own office, because, he says: 'The Commandant was regarded as the lowest form of human existence, a craven coward, and it was generally known he was a heavy drinker without a thought for the suffering in his own self-made concentration camp. It was common knowledge in the camp that the Commandant was seldom sober.'

A group of a hundred mutineers had crashed into the midst of an officers' meeting and summarily ordered them to their feet.

'We were armed, but we did not require to use our weapons. The officers meekly obeyed. We bundled them outside and locked them up in the guardroom next door. We then piled brushwood and trestles round the wooden hut.'

97

It was a succinct ultimatum — half an hour to give an undertaking to improve the soldiers' lot or be burned alive. It took less than ten minutes for an officer to call out a surrender to the terms stated. As Reynolds puts it, 'Like the cowards they were, they quickly capitulated.'

But their ordeal was not yet over. The mutineers then loaded Commandant Thomson and a dozen officers into two trucks and set off with them down the road to the bridge over the River Canche. The little convoy covered the half-mile from the commandant's office at a slow pace so as to give the cheering men lining the route a good view of what was going on. On the bridge the two lorries stopped. There was a moment of silence, then the trucks tipped up and slid the top echelon of the British Army's No. 1 Base over the parapet and into the river — another incident unrecorded in the official diary. By the time Thomson and his senior officers hit the water and were swimming for their lives, the banks of the River Canche were crowded with hundreds of men, yelling and hooting derisively.

From that moment the mutiny spread like wildfire. Sapper David Paton, No. 49479, Royal Engineers, from Dundee, was caught up willy-nilly in the advances by the mutineers into Étaples:

'You were pushed out whether you wanted to or not. Thousands and thousands of us crashed down on the bridges over the railway. You had to go with the crowd. If you had tried to turn round you would have been trampled to death.

'At the bottom of the hill, on the south side of the railway, there were rows of soldiers with fixed bayonets, but if they had tried to stop the mobs getting into Étaples, they would have been crushed to death as well, so they just downed their weapons and went with us. There was no other way they could have gone. There was nothing else they could have done. I can remember the noise now as we went roaring down the hill. The shouting was deafening.

'Hundreds went off to Paris Plage, and it was two or three days before they came back. I heard that a lot never came back.'

Lucien Roussel was a boy of fifteen, helping out in his mother's shop in Étaples town square when the wave of Scots, Australians and English hit them.

'The British troops stormed into the town like real savages, grabbing or destroying everything in their path. They took over the square for days on end. It was black with troops.

'There were bloody incidents at the station, shooting, beatings up, vehicles being set on fire. The rebels took prisoner one of the officers responsible for the camp, locked him up in a slatted wooden cage and paraded him around Étaples on the back of an open lorry.

'I saw a patrol with a number of officers set upon by the mutineers on the Canche bridge. All of them were thrown into the water. Just at that moment a military police lorry arrived on the bridge. The driver, seeing what was happening, tried to reverse, but he was trapped by rebels coming up from behind.

'The two men in the front of the lorry and the four in the back all got the same treatment — into the river. Then the lorry was set on fire.'

An Étaples photographer, Achille Caron, also remembers moments of terror at the station: 'I saw a cavalry officer going at full gallop down the rue de Rosamel with a mob of soldiers in full pursuit.'

The town of Étaples was hopelessly out of control, but in the camp some officers acted to try and stop the situation collapsing completely. They were helped by the construction of the camp. Each infantry base depot was wired in as a self-contained unit on either side of the road. There were usually only one or two gates.

The East Yorkshires were one of several battalions where the officers acted firmly and fast. Senior NCOs were armed and put on the gates. All the men were routed out of their tents and the canteen hut and stood to. The officers did not feel confident enough to risk using their men against the rioters.

'So they kept us on the move,' says Private Jack Musgrove of Dinsdale Avenue, Kings Road Estate, Wallsend-on-Tyne.

'Invented any sorts of jobs for us, so we didn't sit around and conspire. But no one was allowed out of the IBD except the canteen men like myself to g t food. That went on for five days.'

Some officers were more venturesome. Two marched up to Corporal Reynolds's group and started to read out the sonorous terms of the Riot Act and the Army Act, ending each sentence with the invocation, 'The Penalty for this is Death.'

'We just shouted them down,' says Reynolds. 'Their copies of the Acts were just snatched from them and burned.'

As Sunday night drew on the only real sign of authority came from an officer of the Durham Light Infantry. In parade-ground style he turned out fifty of his troops with fixed bayonets and marched them to the main road through the camp. It was the start of a strange three-day gavotte. Private Musgrove, on canteen detail for the East Yorkshires, saw it with astonishment:

'It was like the grand old Duke of York. The Durhams would stand at the bottom of the hill, with their backs to the railway, all of them with fixed bayonets, with an officer out in front, his sword drawn. At the top, which was less than a quarter of a mile away, the Scots gathered in a large group and slowly marched down the hill. The Durhams started up the hill towards them, and then the Scots would break into a trot whereupon the Durhams withdrew to the bottom. The Scots would then take a little rush at them, daring the officer to shout, "Fire." Of course, had the officer done this there would have been a slaughter on the hill, and things were bad enough everywhere else without that. Then there would be a short lapse with both sides standing there staring at each other before the officer shouted "Charge." The Scots then started back up the hill to regroup, the Durhams would retreat and the same performance would begin all over again.

'The Durhams were scared to go too far because the Scots were also armed with rifles, but they did not have bayonets.

It was an endless cat-and-mouse game that was still going on two days later when I went out for more food.'

The rebel Scots had no real quarrel with the Durhams. It was the Military Police who were to feel the full weight of the troops' hatred in the first twenty-four hours. The military police compound at the bottom of the hill was the first target of the Scots and the Australians after news of Corporal Wood's death spread. The police personnel never stood a chance. Most of them broke out and fled towards the railway station and the town.

'The police huts were shattered,' says Jack Musgrove. 'The windows and doors were smashed and off their hinges. Several huts were burning. There was nothing left.'

Several Red Caps were thrown out of first-floor windows. Another group was trapped on the railway bridge and thrown over on to the lines. As dusk fell, a grim manhunt developed among the sidings and cattle-trucks around Étaples station. Two policemen were cornered by a group of Australians who hammered their heads to pulp against the troop trucks waiting at the station. As one frightened French train driver tried to pull out of the station, an Aussie climbed on to the tender and threatened to beat his head in with a lump of coal.

Private W. E. Beane, who now lives at 2 Low Road, Lessingham, Norwich, was with the Royal West Surreys, and was shut in a camp opposite the Scots:

'We were just ordered to stand by. Shooting went on all night, a lot of it. The Scots went right into the base head-quarters looking for military policemen.'

Out in the sand-dunes, Aussies were hunting down the Red Caps and Canaries with Lewis machine-guns, according to Private Joseph Perks of 24c Hebrides Drive, Mill o' Mains, Dundee.

Private Bill Ellett of 23 Valentine Parker Court, Greenhoe Place, Swaffham, Norfolk, had just arrived wounded in hospital at Étaples that night:

'I was only half-conscious. It was the middle of the night. Suddenly the orderlies came along and put our kit on us.

101

We were put on stretchers and hurried out and down to the railway. They just stacked us there in the dark for hours. We thought the Germans had broken through. I remember the shooting and the noise, and then eventually we were put into hospital trucks and taken off to Trouville.'

Yet, according to the commandant's diary, all had been quiet from 10 p.m.

The dawn of Monday was to do little to help Commandant Thomson's Nelsonian view of events. Much of the camp had been abandoned by many of his officers. There was not a military policeman to be seen. But the instructors up at their own camp in the Bull Ring, three miles away, were as yet unscathed.

Those officers who had maintained control of the troops in their own IBD compounds, now attempted to keep the situation as normal as possible. They marched them out for the usual training in the Bull Ring.

Private Phil Chester of the Northumberland Fusiliers, living at 2 Crane Close, Cranwell Village, Sleaford, Lincolnshire, after retiring from thirty years of working at the near-by RAF College, was there:

'The moment you got to the Bull Ring the routine was you fell out and sat on the sand until the instructors came. This particular morning when they told us to get up, nobody moved. We just kept sitting. It was truly an amazing sight to look around and see thousands and thousands of men just sitting there silently. I don't know how it happened, really. I don't remember anything being said about it beforehand.

'There were sergeant-majors, corporals and instructors by the hundreds, all shouting to us to get to our feet. Not a man moved. You could see that the NCOs were flummoxed. There was nothing they could do. No particular group had activated us. It was just as if each man had reached the same decision at the same moment. For two hours they tried every threat and every piece of persuasion they could think of. But

102

nothing happened, nobody stirred. We just went on ignoring them, even laughing at them sometimes.

'In the end they got us up by promising us we could go back to camp, have a day's rest. By that time the sit-down had lasted two hours.'

Back at the camp, the sit-down troops were given a meal, and when they had finished eating they heard, for the first time ever at Étaples, this question, 'Any complaints?' Phil Chester and his mates were so astonished that they celebrated by bursting through the railway-bridge pickets into Étaples for a cup of after-lunch coffee.

General Thomson's diary contains no reference to this mass defiance three miles up the road. He had troubles enough nearer home.

Troops created disturbance in evening.

Owing to police being unable to cope with situation, Major J. Henderson, O.C. No. 25 I.B.D. was ordered to take charge of town of Étaples and to command any guards and picquets. General Officer Commanding Lines of Communication, Asser, visited Étaples in the morning and issued instructions.

Orders were given that all officers were to be present in their Depots from 5.30 p.m. to 10.00 p.m. A Board of Enquiry sat to collect evidence as to the occurrences on 9th September. At 4.00 p.m. bodies of men broke through the picquets into the town and held noisy 'meetings'. During the afternoon and evening several motor cars were interfered with.

A picquet of 2 officers, 100 other ranks from the Lewis Gun School, Le Touquet, was sent to Paris Plage. There was no disturbance nor was any damage done there.

At 6.30 p.m. a mob of 200-300 proceeding along the River road towards Detention Camp were met and addressed by the Base Commandant, and were led by him, assisted by Major White, Major Dugdale, Assistant Provost Marshal, and Captain Strachan A.P.M. back to camp. On No. 1 Bridge a crowd of 1,000 were collected.

103

They were also addressed by the Commandant, and began to disperse, and were evidently from their temper not out to make further trouble.

About 8.00 p.m. another small party of about 100 attempted to get at the Field Punishment Enclosure (where they thought police were hidden). This party was spoken to by the Commandant and dispersed quietly.

At 9.00 p.m. Major Cruickshank, saw a crowd of 100 opposite Town Station. They thought there were police in the station and tried to enter. They were almost immediately persuaded to return to camp.

The demeanour of all crowds towards officers was perfectly good.

Thomson had cause enough to know that the last sentence, at least, was the reverse of the truth. For he had personally encountered a new spirit of organization and leadership, and the first whiff of politics which was turning the Étaples affair from a mass outburst of anger into a determined mutiny.

The mutineers who had not returned to base on the Sunday night had instinctively made their way to link up with the permanent deserters who flourished in the woods around Paris Plage, most of them under the patronage and guidance of Percy Toplis, whom they now nicknamed 'The General'. Mr William Stephens, of Elsynge Road, Wandsworth, London, a Ministry of Social Security official, school governor and Battersea Trades Council vice-president before his retirement ten years ago, was at Paris Plage when the mutineers and the deserters joined forces on the Monday morning. As a private in the Bedfordshire and Hertfordshire Regiment, he was an orderly in one of the hospitals at Paris Plage. He remembers seeing Toplis's name on wanted posters in the area:

'If he was a villain then he was not the only one around Étaples. Maybe he too was tired of being humiliated, deprived, brutalized and treated like a dog. We had all got tired of being treated with less consideration than that given to the horses.'

It was a strange council of war which convened under the dripping wet poplar trees on the morning of Monday, 10 September. The fine weather of the previous day had given way to a steady drizzle, but to warriors accustomed to fighting through mud and blood, these were not uncomfortable conditions. What they were suffering from that morning, as they squatted on the wet grass to discuss their next move, was a common hangover.

The clear-headed Toplis, fresh from an overnight stay in the Hôtel des Anglais where he had posed as an officer just back from the line on leave, had to do most of the thinking for them. The delight of the deserters was boundless when they heard that the Military Police were no more. They were eager to show their gratitude, and, assured that the coast had been quite literally cleared, they offered to return to Étaples with the mutineers to take part in day two of the mutiny, under Toplis's leadership.

This weird, mixed bag of disaffection and desertion started marching on Étaples in the late afternoon. They were about 1,000 strong, and they swung along the coast road, back to the scene of Sunday's triumph. Free at last from the fear of arrest, Toplis boldly led his column of deserters from the front. Before they got to the River Canche bridge they merged and then split up into four separate groups, each numbering over two hundred and each group containing some of the deserters. They hoped that in this manner they would be able simultaneously to cause maximum harassment at different points.

Toplis felt he had a clear duty. He headed his mob straight for the detention compound and released the prisoners, about fifty of them. The Toplis troops met with only token resistance from prison guards, who put up a show at struggling, but made no attempts to use their guns.

Madame Andrée Dissous of Étaples was one of several Frenchwomen who used to sell cigarettes and confectionery to the troops from two-wheeled stalls which were pushed along the road to the Bull Ring. During the half-hour midday break, orange chocolates were very popular with the soldiers. Madame Dissous remembers Toplis's bold stroke well:

'I saw the 200 or so men just march up to the compound gates, issue some threats, and the next thing the prisoners, with their shaven heads, came tumbling through the gates.'

Sergeant-Major Gray of the Gordon Highlanders saw it too:

'The Provost Marshal was thrown down the railway embankment on the way.'

By now Thomson was desperate. He took to the back seat of his long, open staff car on a tour of the areas of the camp that he had never seen before, stopping off wherever mobs of mutineers were gathered to deliver speeches that started off in a blustering manner, but finished in conciliatory fashion when he saw that threats were not going to work.

By 6.30 on the Monday evening, when Thomson ran into the Toplis mob on the river road, the much-shaken, confused general thought that they were on their way to raid the detention camp when in fact they had already been there. He was attempting to close the door of an empty stable. His car had to stop because Toplis and his men were blocking its route. Thomson stood up in the back only to have his opening sentence drowned in a storm of abuse. He got as far as, 'How dare you call yourselves soldiers, British soldiers...' when the mob closed in on his vehicle and started to rock it violently. He was forced to sit down again.

Toplis had dressed for his part. That is to say, this was one of the few occasions when he was actually attired in a private's uniform and not that of an officer. He held up his hand, signalling for silence from his followers. 'What a sight it was to see the commanding officer there with tears in his eyes begging of us to let this trouble subside,' recalls a Lancashire Fusilier, George Souter of Ardwick, 'and appealing for us to keep up the tradition of the British Army.'

The sight of the ashen-faced general, sitting now in the back seat, encouraged Toplis to climb on the running-board and dictate the terms for ending the mutiny. It was for

Toplis, of course, an entirely academic exercise since he had no intention of enduring the Étaples base in any shape or form. He was simply revelling in the revolution. The revolt would end, he told Thomson, only when the town of Étaples was thrown open to the troops, when the Bull Ring had been closed, the military police removed and food and general conditions improved. Thomson turned to make his chauffeur drive on, but he was forced to hear out the private's demands.

He made no reply at that moment, but in the end he would be forced to concede every condition Toplis had laid down. It had been a short, sharp speech, and after he had delivered it, Toplis stepped down from the car and ordered his men to clear the way for it to continue.

He next selected a deputation of five, himself included, to call on the soldiers' champion, Horatio Bottomley, who by chance had arrived to stay at Étaples's Hôtel des Voyageurs while writing a series for his paper *John Bull*. There Toplis repeated the demands to Bottomley, plus an additional one that army pay should be increased. (That too would come to pass.)

By Monday evening, with all training stopped, no police, the mutineers in control of the camp and reinforcements piling up at Folkestone but unable to move, the army had to face the fact that the situation was out of control. Worse for Haig was the nightmare that this sedition might be imported to the front line. The decision was taken that troops — and reliable troops — would have to be pulled out of the forward areas and sent to quell the mutiny.

As the urgent messages went to and fro between Étaples and Haig's headquarters on the Monday night, violence was once again spilling into the streets of the town. Pierre Durigaieux, later to become the town doctor at Étaples, lived in a house behind the town hall, next to the British officers' club. Events, he says, had taken an even more ugly turn:

'Soldiers were attacking women all over the town. I saw

107

them — and some of the women were not so young — trying to climb over high garden walls to get away from the men. But one girl, a fisherman's daughter, did not get away. She was raped by one soldier on the pavement near my house while other soldiers looked on. The attack took place near her home, and her father rushed out with a harpoon and plunged it into the soldier's back.

'Eventually an officer on horseback came into the square to address the mobs. He backed his horse on to the Town Hall steps and started talking to them from there, but he was wasting his time. Those mutineers who were not drunk did not bother to listen to him. The more he shouted the more they screamed. One drunken man staggered into the side of the officer's horse, and the officer leaned down to hear what the drunk was saying. As he did so, the soldier pulled out a knife with a curved blade and slit the officer's throat open from ear to ear. When he fell from the horse there was terrible pandemonium and I ran away to avoid being crushed.

'Throughout the night there were lorries rattling through the town with machine-guns mounted on the back, hunting for officers and police.'

Madame Dissous says:

'A senior officer — we thought it was their commander, but we might have been mistaken — was forced by the rebels to get on his horse and come to the square. Other officers were obliged to walk behind him, and when they all got to the square the officer on the horse made a speech in which he promised better conditions for the men. But I know that before this happened some officers were killed at the bridge in the town.'

On the morning of Tuesday the 11th, the British Army was having to face up to the disaster which threatened it. Brigadier-General Horwood, Chief Provost Marshal of the Armies, was sent post-haste to Étaples. By now Thomson felt that the only way out was to bring in outside troops. Horwood had already been told he could have 700 crack troops from the 1st Honourable Artillery Company. But for

Thomson that was not enough. He wanted the Cavalry. Horwood agreed. But the Cavalry were not so keen to come and polish the sabres, which had rusted in their scabbards throughout the war, on the necks of their comrades-in-arms. There ensued a classic sequence of army diversionary tactics, recorded in Thomson's diary:

> At 1.30 p.m. 9th Cavalry Brigade were rung, but owing to a mistake by telephone operator, call was put through to Cavalry Corps. 2 squadrons, 15th Hussars from Frencq were asked to be held in readiness to move. No answer could be given by Cavalry Corps Headquarters as the Corps Commander was out.
> At 2.00 p.m. Staff Captain Wells motored over to Frencq and told the O.C. 15th Hussars what duties would be required from them in the event of authority being given for their use.
> At 2.30 p.m. Cavalry Corps rang up. They required G.H.Q. authority for the use of Cavalry. Line of Communications communicated with G.H.Q. and about 4.00 p.m. a message, telephone, was received to say G.H.Q. would *NOT* authorise use of Cavalry.

By now a despairing note is entering Thomson's record of events:

> About 4.00 p.m. men again broke through the picquets on the bridge, went through Étaples, broke through the picquet on the River Canche bridge, and went towards Paris Plage. None of the picquets made any determined effort to prevent these men.

And the Cavalry were still not on their way. Thomson made some half-hearted attempts to appease the mutineers.

'We were told that all parades had been suspended,' recalls Private Joe Perks. 'We were even more amazed when we were told that we could draw more than our shilling

109

a day. We were told we could draw as many francs as we liked — within reason.'

Wednesday, 12 September, was to be crisis day for Thomson, Toplis and the British Army. Three days of determined rebellion had made it impossible to dismiss the uprising as a mere explosion of anger, or the effects of drink, or the New Zealanders giving vent to frustration — all explanations which Thomson had come up with. It was impossible for Haig to countenance an impasse across his main route for reinforcements to the front. The battle for Passchendaele was due to start in eight days. There had to be a showdown.

Inside the camp all authority had by now been abdicated. Confused attempts had been made to ship the unaffected troops out to the front by train, but now, as Joe Perks and David Paton remember, the Scots just loafed about. There were no signs of officers or senior NCOs, no attempts to impose any duties — simply extra pay and extra food.

Commandant Thomson had an uncomfortable morning. The French Chef de Gendarmerie for the whole northern district arrived. There was a noisy Gallic scene ending only when Thomson assured him that the British police chief, Captain Strachan, had been fired and that loyal troops were on the way. The gendarme chief and his military colleague, Colonel Vallée, departed with assurances that the riotous assaults on French civilians would stop.

Meanwhile Toplis and the rebel Scots leaders were not having it all their own way. Toplis's demands of the Monday afternoon had still not been conceded. Sooner rather than later the authorities would bring in the machine-guns. Even if they gave way, there was no possible warranty against the sanctions of the firing squad.

The first fury of the mutiny had lapsed. There were anxious, unending meetings all over the camp — even talk of soviets. Some were for quitting while they were ahead. One Cameron Highlander, Ivan Lyon, now of Old Greenock Road, Bishopton, Renfrewshire, stood on a table at a meeting in a camp canteen, pleading with his fellow Scots to

110

stop the revolt. He argued, wrongly as it transpired, that nothing would be achieved. But the men were not to be swayed. Lyon went out and buried the 150 rounds of ammunition he had in his possession in the sands on the beach.

At three o'clock Thomson, in despair, saw a thousand men brush contemptuously past the pickets and march off to the pleasures of Paris Plage. He decided to make a last personal attempt to turn the tide. Once again he called round his open staff car and drove slowly up towards the mutiny headquarters in the Scots IBD. A meeting was still in progress, but the news of Thomson's arrival ended it abruptly.

'All the Scotch crowded round,' says Jack Musgrove. 'In fact they were going to pull him out of the car. They wanted guarantees before they would settle the rebellion. They had to keep all the police away, close the Bull Ring, open up the town of Étaples. The general just stood there. And suddenly it was all granted. Just like that.'

Faced with the bitterness and determination of the mutineers, Thomson collapsed. Toplis and his followers had won.

Written Orders were posted round the camp saying that Étaples would be open until 10.00 p.m. All troops would henceforth go straight through to the front without any training at the Bull Ring. The police would not return.

Ironically, Thomson got back to his office to find the message he had hoped for waiting for him — but too late. The 19th Cavalry Hussars were ready to move with machine-guns at an hour's notice. And the 1st Honourable Artillery Company, with 360 men under Lieutenant-Colonel Cooper, would be arriving at 6.30 p.m.

That night, Colonel Cooper took over all the security duties at Étaples from Thomson's staff. He acted with decision. First Thomson's concessions were confirmed. Then, hemmed in by his column of troopers, carrying loaded rifles with fixed bayonets, Cooper set out on a horse-back patrol of the entire base. Wherever more than fifty mutineers were gathered, he stopped and again read out the Riot Act and the Army Act.

When he withdrew for the night to a compound on the other side of Étaples, Cooper was not reassured by what he had seen. There was no attempt to corral the troops that night. But on Thursday morning the High Command finally determined on a show of strength. The 2nd Army was ordered to send two tough battalions, the 1st Royal Welsh Fusiliers and the 22nd Manchesters.

Private W. Harrop, who now lives at 102 Houghton Lane, Swinton, Manchester, was with the Manchesters:

'We had moved from Bullicourt in the Hindenberg Line in August and arrived in the Ypres area prepared to go into action. Then we were suddenly moved to the nearest railhead in secret and entrained for Étaples. None of us knew where we were going until we arrived there. We were then informed why we were there. As we marched along the road to a site prepared for us it must have created a great impression to see a full battalion arriving direct from the Front, because all was quiet for the three days we had there on Stand To orders.'

At last, on Thursday night, Thomson was able to record a minor victory.

Some 200 men broke out of camp this evening, but were most of them back in camp by 10 p.m. Two of the ring-leaders were injured by entrenching tool handles whilst trying, unsuccessfully, to force the picquet of the 1st H.A.C. at Three Arch Bridge. All ammunition was today collected and sent to Ordnance, and is only issued in future daily as required for reinforcements proceeding up the line.

On Friday, the 14th, Thomson wrote:

Police were re-instated, but with an entirely fresh body of police, and took over in place of guards and picquets previously detailed. The situation is well in hand...

One company of the H.A.C. were held in readiness in the town with the remainder in reserve. One company, Royal Welsh Fusiliers, mounted a guard over the Detention Compound. The remainder of the two Infantry Battalions were held in readiness to act as required. Fifty to sixty men broke out of camp but were arrested in Étaples.

One hundred foot police and fifty camp police of the Étaples Police left today for other stations. This completed the transfer of the original Étaples police.

Friday night was a joyous night for the mutineers. The hated police had been sent packing. Saturday morning brought rapture. Thomson capitulated further. The town of Étaples was thrown open without reservation — a fact the general grudgingly recorded in a sentence sandwiched between records of heavy gun replacements for the front.

By Saturday afternoon and evening, the rioting in the streets had given way to singing and dancing. The victorious rebels stood shoulder to shoulder, as they had done throughout, in Étaples square and sang 'Keep the Home Fires Burning'.

The two main brothels, fetchingly named Le Jardin d'Eden and 290, whose customers until then had been exclusively officers, reduced their prices for the new clients. La Comtesse, dressed all in black, put on a show of private enterprise by driving into the middle of the throng in her horse-drawn landau, cracking a long whip as she announced where she could be contacted.

The *estaminets* had recovered quickly from the pounding received the previous Sunday and throughout the week. They threw open their doors, or what was left of their doors, like the town itself, to the ecstatic but now orderly, well-conducted hordes.

On 20 September, the battle for Passchendaele began, claiming the lives of many of the erstwhile mutineers. On 22 October, after a decent interval, Brigadier-General Andrew Thomson was sacked. But, in between, the army

113

determined that there would be a reckoning with the ring-leaders of the rebellion.

In the middle of the mutiny, Haig had made what seemed an extraordinarily stupid and spiteful decision which threatened for six months to blow a huge hole in the hush-up he carefully created. Without explanation, he had issued an order that the forces' sweetheart at Étaples, Lady Angela Forbes, was to be sent back to England. Not until one of his junior commanders, General Fowke, was subsequently confronted by the redoubtable and indefatigable Lady Angela, demanding with pencil and notebook in hand an official reason for her deportation, did the Commander-in-Chief lamely let it be known that he considered she 'was not a good influence with the troops'.

At 41, Angela Forbes, who had been a high-society beauty of her day, was a leading member of the British aristocracy who had abandoned a whirlwind life of rich gaiety for one of great personal sacrifice and service behind the British lines. She had nursed war-wounded in Paris hospitals at the start of the war, and later founded an organization known as British Soldiers' Buffets at Boulogne and Étaples, months before the Expeditionary Force or YMCA canteens put in an appearance at either of these places.

Before the arrival of General Thomson as commandant, she had succeeded, in the face of much official resistance, in establishing her big tea-and-bun hut in the middle of the camp. Until her arrival the Bull Ring trainees had struggled on without a midday break or a meal. Angela had worn down the opposition to the point where she personally served the troops with cups of tea half-way through their long and terrible Bull Ring day.

Grateful troops used to send her letters of thanks from the front line, and when the news broke of her fight to stick to her self-appointed post, she received many messages of encouragement.

114

The high-born Angela had been a strong supporter of Sir John French, and when he was replaced by Haig she had become an open critic of the new commander-in-chief. She was highly regarded and much loved by some officers and all the soldiers, but was looked upon askance by the Montreuil GHQ. She was far too *avant garde*, much too outspoken and too 'well connected'. She was also a cigarette-smoking divorcée who entertained officers to dances in her Le Touquet villa. Her servants were actually intercepted in the streets by representatives of GHQ and questioned about the identity of her guests.

Haig's edict had not been the first attempt to oust her. She had resisted an earlier effort by the War Office to amalgamate her private-enterprise canteens with those of the YMCA, whereupon an official of the association, prompted by jealousy at the popularity of her huts, reported her as having been seen smoking in public in a Boulogne hotel. There were further complaints that she had been heard swearing and that she rejected all forms of uniform in preference for gaily coloured jumpers and skirts. Clearly, Angela was no angel except in the eyes of the common soldier she tirelessly served!

One of the people who spied on her was Assistant Provost Marshal Strachan, who was directly responsible for the Étaples Military Police. It was her contention that the cruel conduct of the military policemen was but a reflection of the crudity of their chief, who, when he was not reporting on her activities, was continually paring his nails with a pen-knife in her presence! She complained about Strachan to General Plumer.

Among Angela's officer friends was General Asser, with whom she had spent a merry evening drinking in the New Year of 1917 in the deserted dining-room of the Meurice Hôtel in Boulogne; and Asser was one of the High Command sent to Étaples to try to control the mutiny nine months later. To the great delight of his drinking companion, Asser selected Strachan as one of the first to be sacked. GHQ tried to reinstate the assistant provost marshal, but Asser was adamant: Strachan was out for good.

Yet even Asser was powerless to intervene when Haig viciously retaliated by selecting Asser as his personal messenger to Angela with the notice to quit the country. In support of Haig in this move was Adjutant-General Macready, another of Angela's enemies.

In the immediate aftermath of the start of the mutiny on 9 September, at least 10,000 soldiers were rushed away from Étaples and up the line in an effort to stop the rebellion spreading. And the supreme irony of Angela's situation was that at the very moment she was told to go, she was catering for both the needs of men and authority as never before. Her canteen at Étaples Station was the only one serving tea and sandwiches to the 10,000 who were being hurriedly sent on their way. And when General Asser's car drew into the siding, she was standing exhausted behind the counter with her helpers.

The tall, commanding, and still beautiful head tea lady saw that her friend the general was looking unnaturally grave. She recalled the moment:

'He told me, "I have just come from the AG's office with a message for you."

'I jokingly retorted, "To order me out of France?"

' "Exactly," was his reply.

'I burst out laughing. Then I saw he was really serious and I was dumbfounded. What on earth had happened? I had broken no rules or regulations. I had not the smallest sin on my conscience to give me any clue to his extraordinary message.

'When I asked him why he only shook his head and told me he had less idea than I had.'

Indeed, Angela had played no part in the mutiny. All she had done was to rush out when the shooting started near her hut. She had then found herself being swept downhill to the station in the midst of the incensed mob pursuing the military policemen. The only accusation that could have been levelled against her was that for the first thirty-six

116

hours of the mutiny she had kept her refreshment hut open, and had then been given a safe-conduct escort of Australians through the camp and the town of Étaples. Still accompanied by her Australian bodyguard, she had driven her car at a snail's pace to her Le Touquet villa past thousands of mutineers, all madly cheering for 'Angelina', as she was known.

Angela fought back bitterly against Haig with all the power at her command, and that power was enormous. She was a daughter of Lord Rosslyn, Lord High Commissioner of the Church of Scotland, and a goddaughter of Baroness Burdett-Coutts and Lady Bradford. Heading the list of frequent royal guests at the family's two homes in England and their estate in Scotland was the then Prince of Wales, later King Edward VII. In Angela's childhood, Queen Victoria had also been a guest of the family. The remainder of the visitors' book read like *Debrett's Peerage*.

Flimsy though Haig's case against Angela was, there had been some low cunning behind his action. Haig's desperation was as great as that of General Thomson, who was strenuously seeking to make strong drink the scapegoat for the mutiny. Haig's thinking was that if news of the mutiny was going to break, then the most likely source of leakage would be the highly influential Angela with all her friends in high places. He sought therefore to pin the blame in advance on her unsettling influence among the soldiers. And, in the same bold stroke, to settle an old score born of personal enmity.

The commander-in-chief knew from his spies at Étaples that Angela was fond of repeating in public a politician's description of him as 'all chin and no head'. He knew that she openly referred to him as an obstinate and stupid man who ought to be replaced by a French commander. And while Haig spied on Angela, she kept a close watch on him, noting among his other activities the time that he spent playing golf at Paris Plage. And she, in turn, was well aware that the cavalry frequently played polo on the fields adjoining the golf course. Moreover, Angela was an

117

enthusiastic repository for the many rumours of wild drinking parties and scandalous bedroom scenes in the villas of Le Touquet and Paris Plage after the tennis and golf matches in which officers of High Command competed.

Lady Angela was an exceedingly romantic figure whose voluntary war service was exemplary. In contrast to the high jinks and goings-on in the homes of some of her lady friends in society, Angela's claim was that the only time she had 'gone off the beaten track' was when she and her two young daughters had dined with an officer friend in his billet on his birthday, but even that innocent excursion had been reported back to Haig.

Since Haig had no real case against her, he would, if necessary, simply make one up. Even when he started raking into her past, all that he could come up with was that she had written risqué books, one of which, *Broken Commandment*, had been banned by pre-war libraries because it was regarded as 'highly improper'. It was scarcely enough ammunition to start a fusillade against a formidable opponent, one of whose regular villa guests was the new, young Prince of Wales.

But what troubled Haig even more than the repeated sojourns of His Royal Highness with Lady Angela was the secret news imparted to him by Strachan that one of her guests, a few weeks before the mutiny, had been a regular army battalion commander, Toby Long, son of Walter Long, the most respected voice in the Cabinet and consultant to Lloyd George, Haig's arch-enemy. Disturbed by the lack of officers at the front, young Long had decided personally to investigate widespread complaints that Étaples was not just over-crowded with military police, but was also massively over-staffed by high-ranking officers, who ought to have been up the line. Haig was greatly worried that Angela and Toby Long had been intriguing against him and would between them arrange for a bad report to be sent back to Downing Street.

Happily for Haig, his concern was unneccessary and he had worried unduly. If Toby Long had intended to make a

118

bad report, then it died with him at the front, in the week of the mutiny when the officers were still conspicuous by their absence in the firing line.

Angela's first blast of retaliation against Haig's order that she should quit France immediately went via the War Office in London in a personal letter to Lord Derby whom she had known all her life. She also wrote to another friend, Lord Wemyss. He wrote back to her that he had called on Lord Derby, who had at first made 'some rather veiled accusations against her', but had later withdrawn them. Angela immediately set out from Étaples to London to demand an interview with Lord Derby, but he sent a message refusing to see her until her case had been investigated.

She was dismayed. As she recorded later, she had never thought of this particular acquaintance of her family as a man overburdened with brains, but until then she had thought that he was essentially just. Despite Haig's order to get out of France, and to stay out, she returned to Étaples, and from there to Haig's office at Montreuil, six miles away, where she deliberately parked her car in the space permanently reserved for Haig's own staff car.

Instead of being allowed an audience with Haig, she was ushered into the far from august presence of one of his subordinates, the flaccid-faced Fowke, who squirmed his embarrassed way through an interview in the course of which she further disconcerted the hapless general by writing down his answers to her cross-examination. Among the more grotesque reasons advanced for Haig's dismissal order were:

'A clergyman has heard you say damn.'

'You washed your hair in the canteen.'

The comic interview ended with Angela observing that it was not her habit to swear in front of padres, and, yes, she had washed her hair, but out of sight in the canteen kitchen.

As Angela had determinedly, doggedly remained a voluntary civilian worker throughout the war, Haig technically had no jurisdiction over her other than to order her removal from the war zone as an undesirable presence. And

119

it was this knowledge that spurred her on in her search for justice. She followed up her meeting with Fowke with a letter to Haig demanding sane, relevant reasons for his order. But the commander-in-chief ignored this communication. He also ignored the fact that the Forbes canteens at Étaples Station and the Étaples base continued to function as before, and that Angela went on journeying to and from France without regard for the order, which he did not try to enforce.

It was slowly beginning to dawn on the commander-in chief that he had bitten off a great deal more than he could possibly chew, and that the best course open to him was a return to the one of masterly inactivity that he knew so well. But that was not enough for Angela. She wanted to have the order officially rescinded and her good name cleared. She dragged the case through a reluctant House of Commons into the House of Lords, with selected friends in both Chambers seeking further information about Haig's action. Consoling letters poured in on her from all over Britain and France, and eventually the carefully worded evasive replies culminated in an apologia being delivered in the Lords by Lord Derby, the text and content of which had been dictated by Angela and her friends, Lord Wemyss and Lord Ribblesdale.

Part of the deal was that the Lords Wemyss and Ribblesdale would scrap their prepared speeches attacking the War Office and GHQ, and that they would make no attack on either in the press. Instead they eulogized the good works of Lady Angela.

Another fear which haunted Haig had been ill-founded. Angela's attempts to get a full hearing of the story of the mutiny and its causes had failed. The cover-up had continued. When she next returned to Étaples, awaiting her was a GHQ pass ensuring her freedom of movement all over France.

By then it was February 1918, and Angela felt weary and soured. She tore up the pass and set out to work on behalf of the French soldiers. The British soldiers suffered with their sweetheart. As a result of her enforced and repeated absence in London fighting her case, the Étaples canteens had to close down.

To his charge of a pre-war publishing 'impropriety', Haig had raked up and falsely laid at Angela's door the blame for the eccentric behaviour of one of her society friends who, early in 1915, had taken his pack of hounds up to the front with a view to setting off in pursuit of the enemy. When it was politely pointed out to him that this would serve no useful purpose, he had promptly switched to chasing foxes in the countryside behind the battle areas.

10

The mutiny over, the first target in the sights of authority was Percy Toplis. And one of the crack agents in the British Secret Service was called in to track him down.

On 25 September a sharp-eyed dapper little man on a Triumph motor-cycle could be seen racing south down the Boulogne road to Étaples, driving past the long columns of newly arrived reinforcements from England marching towards the base, continuing victims of the one order General Thomson had not revoked.

The motor-cyclist drove into Étaples and stopped at the Grande-Place, where troops were now free to mix, propped his machine against the town-hall steps and sauntered across the cobbled square to the Sévigné Café. Apart from a few French civilians and the café waiters, he was the only person in the square not in uniform. As he took a seat at a pavement table and ordered a coffee, it began to rain and the café owner sheltered his customers by pulling down a red, white and blue striped awning, newly acquired as a welcoming sign to the army now permitted to pull a seat up to the table.

The motor-cyclist unbelted his black coat, hoisted his goggles on to the peak of his flat cap, removed cycle clips from the legs of a neat blue suit and, for ten minutes, surveyed the midday bustle as troop-laden trams rattled through the town centre.

He finished his coffee, remounted his machine and drove out of the Grande-Place, retracing the route taken by the trams by turning left into the rue o'Billiet, up the steep slope and then roaring down the rue Saint-Pierre through the rue Désiré Deboffé, past the tramway terminal and on into the wide Place du Gare. As always, the square was packed with soldiers waiting to leave for the front. The motor-cyclist dismounted and wheeled the machine through the glum, cheerless ranks to the entrance of the Hôtel des Voyageurs, where evergreen-filled window-boxes faced back across the square to the station entrance opposite.

Agent Edwin Woodhall of the Secret Service was going to lunch alone before taking over as the new chief of Étaples police, a force drawn from servicemen who had been policemen in civilian life. A former cavalryman, Woodhall, pre-war, had had the distinction of being the smallest officer in the Metropolitan Police, but he made up for his lack of stature in other respects. He was hard and tough, with a first-class army certificate in boxing, wrestling and gymnastics to prove it.

He had piercing blue eyes, neatly side-parted black hair and a sharp profile accentuated by a jutting chin. He had been selected for his new task because he had a brain that matched the sharpness of his expression. After only four years in the Metropolitan Police, he had been promoted to Scotland Yard's Special Branch in 1910 when he was only 24. He had guarded members of the Royal Family as well as Winston Churchill and Lloyd George. In 1915 he had joined the counter-espionage department of the Intelligence Section of the Secret Service, based at Boulogne. Part of his job had been to guard the Prince of Wales during the period when the prince had been attached to the General Staff in France. His last task before arriving at Étaples had been to discover how so many prisoners of the élite German regiment, the Prussian Cavalry Guard,

123

were escaping from prisoner-of-war camps around Le Havre.

During the day the German prisoners worked at Le Havre docks, and Woodhall hit on the idea of spying on their movements and contacts from the cabin of a crane. He had supplied himself with papers which showed him to be a discharged English soldier married to a Frenchwoman and working as a civilian labourer. He taught himself to drive a crane and got a job in the docks. And from his position ten feet above the ground he spotted a Belgian labourer passing papers to a German officer. Further investigation showed that the Belgian was an essential link in a prisoner-of-war escape scheme organized from Berlin through Geneva and Paris.

Early in his civilian police career, Woodhall had been forced to correct a tendency to be over-zealous, a fault pointed out to him in the London South-Western Magistrates' Court by the defending counsel, the celebrated Sir Edward Marshall Hall, and the presiding magistrates. But he had not allowed a public rebuke to interfere with his initiative and enterprise, and that was why he found himself in Étaples with the capture of Toplis his first priority. For the teenage ringleader, still hiding in Étaples, Woodhall would be a formidable new adversary.

Most of the mutineers had been moved out of Étaples with the utmost haste once the rebellion was finished and the trains could be used again. By the time Woodhall arrived, many of them were already dead, killed in the new battle which Plumer had launched five days before on 20 September. But Haig's officers were not going to leave it at that. There was going to be some retribution.

No more had been heard of the Army's Board of Inquiry set up after the first day of the mutiny. If they did continue to sit, then they must have been overtaken and overwhelmed by the events that followed. However, on 13 September, Captain F. D. H. Joy and other members of the Intelligence Corps had been moved into the base, an indication that by the Thursday the hunt was on for political agitators who might have played a part in the mutiny.

124

The Secret Service followed within days. Once calm was restored, Thomson had started to retaliate by banning alcohol, and remembering the part played by the New Zealanders, announced that the New Zealand Division alone would continue to be condemned to the rigours of the Bull Ring. For the rest, it was in part for the mutineers a pyrrhic victory, enshrined in the diary note: 'Infantry Reinforcements in future to go straight up to the Front to complete their training.'

There was, of course, neither the time nor the facility for training at the Western Front. A wiser decision would have been to have reorganized the Étaples training schedules so that cruelty and brutality no longer played a part in them. There is no evidence that part of the conditions for a satisfactory end to the mutiny contained promises that there would be no punishment or reprisal. And even if Thomson had made such promises in his moments of extreme embarrassment, it is unlikely that Brigadier-General F. W. Radcliffe, his successor, or other British warlords would feel honour-bound to carry out pledges made by a man they had dismissed.

When assistance from outside reached Thomson and his beleaguered officers, they had started straight away to make street arrests among the mutineers, and the Honourable Artillery Company had helped to mount a guard on the prison compound to prevent a repeat of the Toplis raid. It is known that the mutineers were threatened with death by Lieutenant-Colonel Cooper of the Honourable Artillery Company. The published records leave unanswered questions of how many of those arrested actually faced the firing squad. Over 200 British soldiers had already been executed during the war, often for offences far less serious than those committed at Étaples. In the whole war only three men are publicly admitted to have been shot for the offence of 'mutiny'. The implication from the records is that the executions took place in the wake of the Étaples rebellion.

It is inconceivable that everyone escaped the fate threatened by the British Army at the height of its gravest internal

125

crisis. But there is a Ministry of Defence ruling which forbids the release of information relating to wartime executions until a hundred years after those executions are carried out, a rule designed, it is claimed, to protect the interests and feelings of relatives who might still be alive. This lavish gesture towards the risk of remarkable longevity means that the last word on the subject of the Étaples mutiny will not be written until the records are opened in the year 2017. The one thing certain is that the man Edwin Woodhall was hunting was doubly at risk. Percy Toplis was not only a mutineer, but also a deserter, and both were capital offences.

Woodhall began to trawl through the underground hideouts of the deserters:

'With a large covered lorry about an hour before dawn, and with about eight or nine picked men, we would proceed silently and swiftly to a prearranged rendezvous. Men would be stationed at each entrance of the chalk dugouts to prevent escape in the dark. Then at the point of a revolver I would enter the cave with a flash lamp, and arrest anyone I found.'

But Toplis was never among them.

Like Toplis, Woodhall favoured disguise in any form. At the time the officers' quarters were still being raided, and when one particular set had been burgled repeatedly, he dressed up as an officer's servant to keep watch. This method of detection led to him tracking down a deserter to a toolhouse near Paris Plage lighthouse. The toolshed had been turned into an Aladdin's Cave of goods, to the value of thousands of pounds, stolen from camps in the area.

But tracking down Toplis was to be a lot more difficult. It was well into October before, in the end, he resorted to the simple device of putting up posters offering a £15 reward for information leading to the capture of Toplis. Quickly a tip led twelve kilometres south to the village of Rang du Fliers.

Rang du Fliers straggles beside the rue de Montreuil for a distance of about half a mile, and at the centre of the village are level-crossing gates flanking the Boulogne-Paris railway which cuts across the road at this point. Just over the level-crossing is a dull grey café, then part of the Liberty Hotel, which is now closed. On the bleak morning of the 15th, Woodhall borrowed a horse and approached the village via the cemetery at its western end, dismounted and led the animal along a pathway in the cemetery to a point behind the eight-foot-tall, five-foot-wide sepulchre built by the Garson family to honour its dead.

Set into the vault about half-way down was a figurine of the Virgin Mary, protected by an iron grille above which was the inscription, 'Famille Garson. Ici Repose Le Corps D'Émile Leboeuf. Age De 30 Ans. 7 Juin, 1878.' Woodhall tethered his horse to the grid. In absurd theatrical fashion, he took from his saddle-bag a dog collar, a white shirt and a priest's habit, and, shielded from view by the sepulchre, exchanged his clothes for these garments. He walked a quarter of a mile before turning left into a sugar factory opposite the Liberty Hotel just short of the level crossing.

He then climbed some wooden steps to join two of the new-style Etaples military policemen who had been keeping watch on the hotel and the café on the other side of the street. They could hear the trains for the front rattling over the crossing as they waited for their quarry.

But of Toplis there was still no sign.

Woodhall had been standing by the window, concealed by curtains, for nearly twenty minutes before the penny dropped. His informer had said Toplis would be at the hotel at noon, not that he would be arriving then. Toplis was already there, as a resident in the hotel.

Woodhall arranged for the two policemen to wait and then follow him into the café. After a tense two minutes, they pushed in the door to find a group of bewildered French customers clustering round an English-speaking priest who was holding up a monocled British Army captain at gun-point.

Elated, Woodhall telephoned the Provost Marshal with news of his capture from the *telegraphe poste* next to the sugar factory. Immediate arrangements were made for a court martial to sit the next day to hear the twin charges of desertion and mutiny. But the charges were never levelled. The court never did sit. Again, the army failed to take Toplis's ingenuity into its reckoning.

Toplis, of course, was already familiar with the inadequacies of the prison compound, and when he returned officially under armed escort he could see they still existed. The prison was a stockade erected from huge wooden stakes about ten feet in height, and inside this was a double row of barbed-wire entanglements surrounding several wooden guard-houses. The only armed guards on duty were stationed at the main gate. The compound overlooked the railway, and on the other side it faced the River Canche.

At about 3 a.m. the next morning, a searchlight suddenly picked up a figure in its beam. The shadow for a moment zig-zagged to avoid the rifle bullets, and then was lost. With chagrin, Woodhall recounts the story:

'Unfortunately, during the night, Toplis, with another notorious character who also had the death sentence against him, tunnelled down under the sand of the barbed wire compound and broke out. The escape was daring to a degree, for the compound was situated on the banks of a river, but, nothing daunted, they dashed down the slope of the foreshore, though it was high tide with a swiftly running current, plunged in the river and swam across to the other side and made good their escape into the woods in and around Le Touquet.

'Before the day was out, with a strong posse of armed men, I found the other man in an exhausted state near Berck Plage. But my real man got away, and although I scoured and combed the place for miles, he successfully eluded all the attempts at capture.'

Angry and frustrated, Woodhall turned out the army messenger dogs from the Étaples kennels in an attempt to pick up the trail. They were still barking and baying their way through the woods at noon the following day. By then, Toplis had reunited himself with the uniform of an RAMC private, his real status, and was hitch-hiking his way towards

Boulogne on army transport. The seriously wounded on the next troopship which pulled out of Boulogne harbour, heading back for dear old Blighty, were grateful for the kindness and attention of one particular ginger-haired medical orderly.

Left behind to die from his wounds in an Étaples hospital was the poet Leslie Coulson, who had written 'But a short time to live':

> Our little hour — how short a time
> To wage our wars, to fan our fates,
> To take our fill of armoured crime,
> To troop our banner, storm the gates.
> Blood on the sword, our eyes blood red,
> Blind in our puny reign of power,
> Do we forget how soon is sped
> Our little hour.

11

When the War Cabinet met at 10 Downing Street at noon on Monday, 10 September 1917 — the day after the start of the mutiny at Étaples — the twelfth item on the agenda was 'Disaffection amongst British troops'. It provoked a long discussion which took up most of the meeting.

Had the Cabinet been privy to the situation at Étaples, it would certainly have been item number one. As it was, the discontent they talked about was among soldiers stationed at Shoreham in Sussex. The Cabinet had not been informed about Étaples. It never was informed officially. Though the Lady Angela Forbes affair certainly was to alert individuals like Lord Derby, the War Secretary. It studiously ignored hints such as those contained in a letter from the Bishop of Oxford;¹ this drew attention to mutinous rumblings at Shoreham, but was a curiously guarded communication which was pointing a finger at Étaples as well as Shoreham. The bishop referred to a similar situation at 'another place' and 'elsewhere', and urged that inquiries should be made at 'the other place'. No one, it appears, took the trouble to ask where that other place was. The bishop had written his letter to Lord Curzon and marked it 'Private and Confidential':

I am writing to you as a member of the War Cabinet. It is most probable that what I am to say will be no news to you: and in that case no harm will be done. You will simply destroy my letter.

But it may be otherwise. The subject of my communication is the serious disaffection which appears to exist among the troops, and which is supposed to be widespread. A friend of mine, a sensible and capable layman, who has been working for a year with the Y.M.C.A. at the great camp of Shoreham (Sussex) has just been to see me, full of apprehension of the most serious kind. Another friend, a young officer, has said similar things about another place.

The disaffection is reported as growing rapidly. Its manifestations in the camp I have spoken of, are such as these — refusal to work in the evening without more food — persistent continuous refusal to sing 'God Save the King' in church and in concerts — secession at night of a company out of the camp leaving a placard to say they were going to imitate the Russian soldiers: and more than any of these particular incidents, open sedition in speech with a growing determination to carry it into action.

This information concerns a convalescent camp, where the men are being recovered for renewed service. They have suffered and been wounded, and it seems to be resented that they are under a Commandant who has not left the country.

The grounds of objection appear to be
(i) *Insufficiency of Food* — especially their having nothing after 4.30 tea:
(ii) *Refusal of Leave* — the grounds of this are intelligible: but it is put upon the absence of sufficient railway accommodation. Yet the soldiers see constant empty trains pass along the line, and when they go into Brighton (without a railway pass by walking four miles and 'bus'), they see crowds of trippers who have been brought by train:
(iii) *The low rate of pay* — 'not nearly enough to keep them in cigarettes'.

131

My other friend from elsewhere spoke of the enormous number of deserters they see when they do go on leave.

I daresay you know all this. But I imagine the Officers in Command are not willing to report such things. What I would suggest is that the War Cabinet should send and make careful enquiry in this particular camp and at the other place.

Forgive me if this is all needless.

There was, of course, nothing 'needless' about the bishop's letter as events were to prove. But that part of it relating to 'the other place' was rendered useless. His suggestion that it required on-the-spot investigation was ignored. The Cabinet chose to concentrate on Shoreham. As the minutes of the Cabinet meeting, drawn up by Acting Secretary Lieutenant-Colonel W. Dally Jones, read:

Attention was called to a letter received by Lord Curzon from the Bishop of Oxford, relative to the grave discontent which existed amongst the troops stationed at the Command Depot at Shoreham, the grounds of objection being stated to be insufficiency of food and refusal of leave owing to the absence of sufficient Railway accommodation.

Director of Organisation, Major-General Hutchinson stated that similar reports had been received before the letter from the Bishop of Oxford had been brought to his notice. The grievance as to leave (a) was primarily due to the restrictions in the use of trains running to Brighton, an Order having been issued by the Army Council, as the result of a War Committee decision on the 29th November, 1916, that train-travelling was prohibited and that men going on leave from Shoreham must travel by motor-buses. These, owing to the petrol shortage, had since ceased to run.

Another grievance was the question of pay (b), the low rate of which caused irritation to our men, owing to the fact that Canadian troops, with their high rates of pay, were quartered in their vicinity. A further grievance was the food question (c), for which he thought there was no foundation, as the men had practically the same food ration as if they were camped in France.

He stated that the men stationed at Shoreham were sent there to harden up for further services, after being wounded, or sick, and that their daily work was progressive until they had been rendered fit for service once more.

As regards (a) the War Cabinet requested —

The Army Council to make the necessary arrangements to provide accommodation for the troops going on leave in the trains running between Shoreham and Brighton and vice versa.

With regard to (b) the War Cabinet requested —

The Military Authorities to go into the matter of re-grouping the Convalescent Camps so that Dominion soldiers were not quartered in the same Command Depots with British soldiers.

As regards the actual rate of pay of the latter, the War Cabinet directed the Secretary to put on the Agenda at an early date the Report of Sir Edward Carson's Committee on Increased Rates of Pay for Soldiers.

As regards (c), complaints with regard to food, the War Cabinet were unable to concur with the view expressed by the Military Authorities, that the food ration was adequate, having in view that the men were convalescent, and the suggestion that the dietary was not equal to that consumed by the average working man in England.

They therefore directed —

The War Office to enquire into the food supply not only at Shoreham, but at all Command Depots, and to furnish a report on the subject as soon as possible.

Director of Personal Services, Brigadier-General Childs was of opinion that though there was a certain amount of discontent in certain units it was not in any way general. That the conditions which had been discussed contributed towards discontent, but that the real great cause amongst men at Command Depots was that they were being hardened up for service again at the front, having perhaps been

133

wounded two or three times, whilst there were thousands of fit men in the United Kingdom in protected industries earning very high wages who had never been called up for military service.

He knew that Lord Derby and the Adjutant-General had been lately giving serious consideration to the problem of the wounded soldier, and he thought that he heard the word 'discharge' mentioned.

He added that absence was a somewhat common offence at Command Depots, but that as regards desertion there had been no increase in the percentage. He mentioned that the efforts to create a Workmans' and Soldiers' Council in this country, had been a complete failure so far as the Army was concerned.

The Bishop of Oxford had come out into the open by stating that sedition was at the point of physical rebellion at one of the biggest troop camps in Britain. It seems strange that he did not come completely clean about 'the other place'. The Bishop wanted his letter to be destroyed, an apparently odd request. The probability is that, influencing his nervous approach, was the wish to protect himself and his informants should the information prove incorrect. The Defence of the Realm Act had an entire section devoted to dealing harshly with those guilty of 'spreading false reports and making false statements', especially a report as serious as the one he had embarked upon.

However, if the Bishop behaved in a coy and odd manner, then stranger still was the behaviour of the Cabinet. Although the letter was a peculiar mixture of hesitancy, diffidence and alarm, it was more than a broad hint that matters were seriously amiss at the mysterious 'other place'. It invited, even begged, for further investigation, but none was forthcoming. A whole succession of people — Curzon, Childs, War Office chiefs and members of the Cabinet — either did not spot the obvious warning or decided to ignore the problem in the hope that it might go away.

The bishop's letter had been written on 3 September and

must have been in the hands of War Office officials, as well as in those of Ministers, for the better part of a week. Had someone bothered to lift the telephone, the call would have answered the vital question: what other place? Had that phone call been made, it is extremely unlikely that Brigadier-General Thomson would have ever written in his diary: 'Owing to the police being unable to cope with the situation, Major J. Henderson, officer commanding No. 25 Infantry Battalion Division, was ordered to take charge of the town of Étaples and to command any guards and pickets.'

The War Cabinet that day consisted of Bonar Law, Viscount Milner, Lieutenant-General Smuts and Sir Edward Carson as well as Lord Robert Cecil, the acting Secretary of State for Foreign Affairs, General Sir W. R. Robertson, the Chief of the Imperial General Staff, Vice-Admiral Sir R. E. Wemyss, the Acting First Sea Lord and Chief of the Naval Staff, and Brigadier-General A. W. F. Knox, the Military Attaché to the Russian Embassy.

It would already have been too late by then for them to prevent the mutiny, but it could have been avoided had it not been for the similar neglect shown by many others in the days immediately prior to the Cabinet meeting. The consequences were already proving serious. And, had it not been for a momentous decision at Étaples made late the previous night by Lieutenant Davies — ironically, one of the rebels referred to by the bishop — these consequences could have been completely and bloodily disastrous.

Indeed, the War Cabinet was being less than well served that day of 10 September. Brigadier Childs implied that there was little desertion. Yet newspaper reports of soldiers being charged with desertion were about as common as the crime itself. The method of disguise most favoured by the troops was to masquerade as uniformed officers, thereby greatly reducing the risk of being challenged. Although he may have been the master performer, Toplis did not hold the exclusive copyright to that practice.

In the week of the mutiny, and throughout the entire month of September, Bow Street Court had its fair share of desertion cases and allied crimes. One man was sentenced to six months' imprisonment for wearing the uniform, decorations and badges of a lieutenant-colonel. Samuel Westaway of the East Kent Regiment was collected at Bow Street Court by military escort and taken back to France from where he had deserted. And Merchant Seaman George Douglas, who had swapped the dangerous ocean waves and the U-boat menace for luxury living on land at an army base and then at a naval base in the North of England, received six months' hard labour for posing as an engineer lieutenant of the Royal Navy. He should have gone on wining and dining in the army officers' mess, because it was only after he transferred to the naval base that he was found out. The officer in command there had detected that the gold and purple stripes on Douglas's uniform were not the precise distance apart.

On the Saturday before the 10 September Cabinet meeting, *The Times* had reported the case of Thomas Smith, alias John Hill, alias George Savage, who had returned home in true Toplis style, though with less success.

> The prisoner who was found as a stowaway on board a ship stated that he had been a coal trimmer on a boat trading between this country and Boulogne.
>
> The police now said the man's real name was Thomas Smith. He had deserted the Army in France and got aboard the ship at Boulogne and been found at Gravesend. He was sentenced to three months' imprisonment with hard labour and ordered to be handed over to the Military Authorities afterwards.

This type of case was being repeated over and over again in courts throughout the country. An extraordinary hearing took place in the same month at Lambeth Police Court, where Benjamin James Casey, aged 15 (a statistic not disputed by the army), was charged with desertion from the RAMC in France. The magistrate, Chester Jones, said the lad's mother had sent his birth certificate to the authorities two months previously, but no notice had been taken of it.

Casey would have to go with the military escort awaiting him, but Mr Jones did not think the military would keep him.

Young Ben Casey plainly regretted the earlier enthusiasm which had prompted him to lie about his age when he voluntarily enlisted. But if he ever was, in fact, allowed to return to civilian life, then he would have been merely exchanging one form of disillusion and disenchantment for another. For the seeds of discontent were being scattered among the British civilian population as well as the army in the late summer of 1917. In Russia a more clearly defined ideological struggle would lead to the final collapse of the Russian war effort and the October Revolution. The average Briton — both on the home front and in a military sense — was simply tired of the struggle. War-weariness was never more evident than during this particular period.

At home, strict petrol rationing had virtually caused the disappearance of private cars, but the price of bread was one of the biggest grievances. At 1s. a loaf it was more than twice the pre-war price. In addition to the austerity hardships, London and south coast towns were being continually bombed during September, although the worst raid had occurred on 13 June 1917, on London, when 162 people had been killed and 432 injured.

The government had appointed a Commission of Enquiry into Working Class Unrest in June 1917, with instructions to announce their findings within three weeks. The commission found that high food prices, particularly in the north-east, caused most resentment. There was also the belief that these prices were mainly due to profiteering.

Wages had, at their highest, increased by about 40 per cent, but some incomes had not increased at all, while the cost of food had soared by 102 per cent and the cost of living generally by 75 per cent. Beer was weak and housing was poor, the commission reported. And there was a feeling of a loss of confidence, indeed, of a lack of trust, in the government.

In May 1917 the weekly meat ration had been reduced to three-quarters of a pound. Tea and butter rationing had been introduced, and — shades of Shoreham — rail services had

137

been drastically cut while rail fares had doubled. Newspapers had doubled their prices. Housing conditions in some areas were described as scandalous. As if all this was not enough, despair had also set in that the war would never end. Military reports from General Headquarters in France of Allied successes had become highly suspect. They were being judged against the daily death-toll from France. Britain was beginning to believe that it was bleeding to death.

Many newspapers, *The Times* included, listed the names of dead officers in separate columns under the heading, 'Roll of Honour'. Death below the rank of lieutenant meant being listed, often on a different page, under the title, 'Losses in the Ranks'. There was also strong resentment at the rigorous manner in which the Conscription Acts were being applied by an over-zealous military authority. An example of this was reported in *The Times* of Saturday, 8 September:

At Camberwell Tribunal, the Military Representative applied for the withdrawal of a conditional exemption certificate granted to a greengrocer aged 36, who had nine children, eight of whom were under 12 years old.

The Military Representative — You seem a bit doubtful as to their ages?

Applicant — It wants a bit of keeping in your head.

The Military Representative held that the man's family would be better off financially if he joined the Army as his weekly profits were only 50s.

Mr. S. Sayer said this was a one-man business, with nine children dependent on it. They had given the son of a German, passed for general service, three months' exemption, that morning, and he saw no reason why they should treat an Englishman in a different way.

The man was granted three months' exemption. The Military Representative said that he would appeal against the decision.

The suicide rate was escalating. Lilian Hazard, 43, wife of Louis Hazard, insurance clerk, Dyncourt Gardens,

138

Upminster, Essex, was one of the many who had had enough. She was found, with her throat cut and a razor by her side, in a clump of rhododendrons in Brookwood Cemetery close to the grave of her sister. Her husband told the inquest that her nerves had been shattered by air-raids and general war.

General Thomson recorded that, in France, Captain F. Roche and Second-Lieutenant J. E. Kinna had tried, but failed, to find a less drastic way out of their troubles. Both had died of self-inflicted wounds in hospital at Étaples. This was an all-too-common entry in the general's diary. Although suicide among the fighting soldiers was also on the increase, it was not always the motive behind self-inflicted wounds. If they went undiagnosed as such, they were often the means of being invalided away from the fighting. The usual method was to shoot off some fingers or toes, but in their attempts to pretend that they were genuine war wounds, many men went even further. Often the wounds were so serious that they did not respond to treatment, and this was believed to be so in the cases of Captain Roche and Second-Lieutenant Kinna. Their calculated risk had not paid off.

In the first week of September, 57-year-old Ziegfried Franz Paul of Delverton Mansions, Gray's Inn Road, London, dramatically demonstrated that he still preferred life in depression-laden England. Ordered to return to his native Germany, he poisoned himself and left a suicide note, saying, 'Being forced to choose between going to Germany and death, I chose the latter.'

In a sad, perverse way, the story of Ziegfried Paul's death — headlined in newspapers throughout Britain — fleetingly reminded the population that though life had become very difficult, there were some who judged it to be worse in the land of the enemy. In August 1915, the weekly *John Bull* had become the British serviceman's mouth and earpiece when its editor, Horatio Bottomley, pledged, 'No case of hardship or injustice, no instance of beggarly treatment or mean cheese-paring, shall go unchallenged and unremedied.' And although the average British Tommy's trust in *John Bull* was diagnosed as a pathetic faith by many, there was no doubt that the reported complaints, both from the battlefields and base depots, met with some positive response, helped morale a little and kept the complacency and indifference of authority in check.

In September 1917, Bottomley decided that the moment had come for him to lighten the deepening gloom still further, both at the front and at home. He became a crisis · crusader. He received special permission to tour the battlefields of France during the first two weeks of September, and his dispatches, date-lined 'Somewhere in Hell', were so ecstatic and wildly optimistic that in subsequent issues he had to admit he was getting letters from soldiers of the 'Were we at the same football match?' type. The message in Bottomley's first centre-page, four-column spread on 22 September was not only that all was well, it was also that *the war is won, Germany is beaten.* This is part of what he wrote:

And now for what I have learnt. We will have the truth from the trenches, at last. The war is won. Germany is beaten. On every front she is weakening and weakening — and it is now only a question of the psychological moment to strike.

That momentous decision rests with one man — at least, I hope to God it does. If the politicians will kindly keep out of the ring Haig will very soon administer the knock-out blow. *I know what I am saying*: I do not profess to speak as any military expert or prophet. I say that which I have learnt. I mention no names — I disclose no secrets — I abuse no confidence.

From Field-Marshal Commander-in-Chief, right down to the rawest Tommy in the trenches, there is but one spirit — that of absolute optimism and confidence. And there is not a German prisoner who does not tell the same tale. 'Es ist fertig', said everyone of them with whom I talked — 'It is finished'. Russia, of course, has been a big disappointment — but, Russia notwithstanding, *we have won.* But for the fact that our Near Eastern Ally suddenly went mad, there is no question whatever that August

140

would have seen a combined offensive on every front, which here now would have got the Hun on the run. Of course, her temporary defection was a serious blow — but happily, it has not proved a mortal one. Indeed, from some points of view — provided I am right in the assumption that the end is near — the hands of the Allies may have been strengthened by what has happened.

At any rate, I have learned this — that, except for the inevitable delay of the final Offensive, the High Command are in no way distressed by the so-called Russian Revolution, the true nature of which you may take it, is quite understood out at the Front.

Bottomley's repeated and near-hysterical claims in his widely read newspaper that the war was won may have been part of the price he felt was expected, or that he had to pay, for the privilege of dining and wining with General Haig, whom he described as 'a great and shrewd man'.

It may even have been that his prolonged visit to the front — an invitation not extended to other editors of the day — carried an unwritten condition that his reports should contain elements of raging enthusiasm. Authority was desperately seeking to raise the low morale of the period, and this was one of the ways open to it. It was an exercise in propaganda that did not merely fail. It rebounded badly. Even Bottomley's Army Command backers must have felt he had overdone it.

For one thing, there was a main obstacle that all the editor's screams of triumph could not hurdle. And this was the fact that, contrary to Bottomley's version, the war was still going on in its desperate, weary way. Continuing to be confronted with this irrefutable evidence that he had got it wrong, having been challenged by much of his Western Front readership on the grounds of inaccurate and incomplete reporting, and having personally encountered the Étaples mutineers, Horatio Bottomley started to shift his ground. By 6 October he was writing:

I asked the boys to jot down the main matters of complaint; and I think they are summarised under the headings of Leave, Pay, Field Punishment, Military Policing, Short Rations, and Cushy Posts at the back which might be filled by wounded officers and others — thus releasing able men for the trenches.

I discussed these, and other questions, with Sir Douglas Haig and various officers — and I am hopeful that good results may follow.

I have also made it my business, since my return, to see Lord Derby personally upon the subject, and I have his assurance that every legitimate complaint — especially in the matter of Leave — shall receive immediate and sympathetic consideration. And I am certain that he is sincere. At any rate, I am proud to be Tommy's Ambassador.

'Tommy's Ambassador' had listed some of the causes of the Étaples mutiny. But a combination of censorship and his own intense desire to push Haig's line meant that he chose to ignore what he knew about the revolt. However, there was a further change of emphasis in the *John Bull* issue of 13 October where Bottomley admitted that he had been accused by Tommy of 'keeping things back'. He protested:

I should much like to tell you the date at which, and the circumstances in which, in the opinion of Sir Douglas Haig, the war will end.

But to do so would clearly be giving the enemy a hint as to both the time and the nature of the further blows which are in preparation. And I have gone as near as I felt safe in going when I said that nothing has occurred to modify the Field-Marshal's confidence, of a complete, *and early* victory. For the rest, you must read between the lines and look at those other 'Lines' where our boys are making mincemeat of the foe.

Bottomley's change of tense when referring to the state of the war completed his climb-down. The use of the words 'will

142

end', plus a very vague prophecy about a Christmas peace, meant that the growing suspicion of his readers was confirmed. They could settle back again into their state of deep despair. But the talent for self-delusion and the policy of attempting to visit it upon others was not exclusive to Bottomley. The War Cabinet had to keep up its own spirit in those dark days.

It had been the practice of Haig's personal staff when he visited the front, which was far too seldom, to select thin and hungry-looking German prisoners-of-war for him to inspect. Tough, well-nourished, hard-fighting Prussians were kept well in the background, so creating the impression that the German fighting machine was creaking.

Although Haig played along with this little game by pretending ignorance of it, it was precisely the ploy he adopted when General Sir 'Wullie' Robertson, Chief of the Imperial General Staff, and the Prime Minister, David Lloyd George, visited Flanders between 24 and 26 September. As the minutes of the War Cabinet meeting of 27 September recorded, 'The Prime Minister remarked on the poor condition of the German prisoners-of-war he had seen on the 26th instant, and upon the very good spirits which prevailed among all ranks of our own army that he had seen and conversed with.'

Haig had every right not to want the very alarming story of Étaples to leak to the enemy, or even to his own army in general, but he had no justification for concealing information about the state of morale of his troops from the Prime Minister and the Cabinet. The bishop had suspected correctly when he wrote to the Cabinet, 'I imagine the Officers in Command are not willing to report such things.'

However, Haig did have very strong personal reasons for taking the risk that his cover-up from the Cabinet en masse might be found out. Lloyd George was still angling for Haig's dismissal, and seeking support from within the Cabinet towards that end. The Étaples mutiny might have made a platform from which the Prime Minister could have launched a new assault. And Haig knew it.

What he did not know was that he almost certainly owed his continuation in command to the absence of Lloyd George from the Cabinet meeting of 10 September. On that day, Haig, from his headquarters half a dozen miles up the road from Étaples at Montreuil, was restricting himself to setting up an Étaples 'Board of Enquiry to collect evidence as to the occurrences on 9th September'. Confronted with serious unrest at Shoreham and elsewhere, the Cabinet was at that moment contenting itself with resolutions calling for train space for troops on the Brighton run, separation from Dominion comrades, and an improvement in the amount and quality of bully beef. A renowned stickler for detail, the chances were that the Prime Minister would have demanded further information about that 'other place'.

But Haig's luck held. The Prime Minister was again absent when the minutes were approved at a Cabinet meeting on 12 September. And when he visited France and Belgium later in the month, there was no way in which he would be allowed to catch up on the information.

Like the Prussian prisoners, the Étaples mutineers were kept well to the rear on the day. They were not among the high-morale troops whom David Lloyd George 'saw and conversed with'.

12

Brigadier-General Andrew Thomson un-
believably went on to cause the army further heartache after
he was fired from Étaples.

The official reason put out by the High Command for
Thomson's removal from the position of base commandant
and his reversion in rank from temporary brigadier-general
to colonel was 'illness', and in the light of what was known
about his drinking habits, this may have been partially true.
Thomson left Boulogne on 23 October 1917, and went
straight to the Somerset home of his brother-in-law who had
just been permanently invalided out of the army on an
entirely legitimate basis.

Haig had rightly calculated that Thomson would keep
quiet about the true reason for his dismissal. The former
commandant had every reason to do so. Three months later
he got his reward. He was reinstated to his former rank, and
dispatched apparently out of harm's way as commandant of
British prisoners-of-war in neutral Holland. He could hardly
be risked on active service and the army was keen to see him
out of England.

Thomson's new Dutch command was the result of one of
the 'side-shows' of the First World War. The 1,500 British

internees whom he arrived to take over in the northern Dutch university town of Groningen were the remnants of Winston Churchill's ill-starred attempt to save Antwerp from German capture in October 1914: a belated, hopeless, doomed intervention by 6,000 men of the Naval Brigade for which Churchill was subsequently bitterly attacked on the grounds that much prestige was lost by a defeat which was eminently predictable.

In 1914 these men of the Royal Naval Volunteer Reserve, completely without training, had been played on to trains by a brass band at Dunkirk, their only instruction being that of their commandant, Lieutenant-Colonel George Cornwallis West: 'Remember you are British, and I am sure you will give a good account of yourselves.' The Naval Brigade tried to do just that. But their weapons were inadequate, their training non-existent and they arrived too late. They were, moreover, hopelessly engulfed by thousands of fleeing Belgian civilians. Not even a desperate, on-the-spot intervention by the First Lord of the Admiralty himself could save the day.

The astonished troops had encountered their supremo in the midst of confusion on a road outside Antwerp. Churchill had been on his way to confer with Naval Brigade commanders when he was caught up in the maelstrom of fleeing Belgian refugees and British soldiers. He presented an extraordinary sight, dressed in a flowing, dark-blue cloak and yachting cap, as he jumped from his car and vainly tried to disentangle the jumble by yelling orders from a vantage point on an embankment. Not even Churchill's personal presence could stem the retreat from Antwerp. Fifteen hundred members of the Naval Brigade strayed across the border into Holland. There they were interned for the duration.

They lived comfortably enough in comparison with those left to fight on, occupying three large wooden huts known as Timbertown, with adjacent huts serving as bath-houses, recreation hall, workshops. Although they suffered the deprivations common to all long-term prisoners-of-war, together with the acute anxiety caused by the uncertainty of the length of their detention, their fears, frustrations and sense of bitterness were not reflected in the camp's monthly magazine.

But with the arrival of Thomson at The Hague as their guardian angel, all that was to change. Thomson had evidently learned few lessons from Étaples. He was never mentioned by name in the prisoners' periodical, but his remote dictatorship immediately made itself felt. In the June 1918 edition of the camp magazine, under the heading EDITORIAL, the whole of page 1 was a blank with just the one word 'Censored' printed across the middle. Page 2, however, provided some explanation.

We regret having to insert so many blank pages this month but at the last moment the above article, together with the one on the hunger demonstration that took place during May, has been censored. Why, we do not know, for both contained nothing but bare facts and a decidedly moderate record of the 'protest' and the general feeling of the Camp.

While apologizing to our readers, many of whom we know look to us to give a true and concise view of our life here, we trust that they will recognize that our inability to furnish a full account of what has lately happened in our midst is due to the nature of what transpired.

The amazing fact was that the rule of Thomson had provoked another outburst of bitterness and a demonstration of protest. The magazine went on angrily to refer to the 'isolated minority' at the top, whose only help was to offer 'heroic' expressions such as 'Grin and bear it', 'Be British'. The interned troops were hard hit by inflation and inadequate food, and Thomson's empty words produced only resentment. As the magazine commented next month:

The whole atmosphere is pregnant with bitterness. It is idle and wrong to say that the rations are sufficient for the physical needs of developing young men, and it is just as wrong to compare our position with that of the Dutch

147

populace at large. Rationed though they may be, they can augment their allowances with foods and delicacies that are beyond the range of our purses: for most of the Camp's members have to depend upon their one pound a month allotment with which to supplement their scanty rations, while those who are married and possess families are dependent upon less.

The face value of the pound in this country is at present sixteen shillings and four pence, while the cost of food-stuffs has doubled and trebled itself.

And, in October:

We are not whining, and we have no wish to suggest that we are lacking in fortitude and courage, but the common, ordinary obligations we owe to country and self must be consulted and carefully safeguarded.

The extremely serious mood of these editorials threatening further discord and disruption must have got through even to Thomson, in his position as one of the 'isolated minority', and made him glad that the war finally came to an end the following month. With the Armistice, the Naval Brigade at last went home to Britain. Brigadier-General Thomson, on the other hand, took his demobilization and departed for Switzerland with his wife. He would never return to his native country.

13

Armistice Day 1918 in Nottingham was subdued compared with the wild scenes which took place in London, or even in the near-by towns of Derby and Leicester. Practical problems prevented, as the local paper put it, 'the repetition of the orgies associated with the relief of Mafeking'. Many of the pubs had no beer and shut their doors. The street lights were left shrouded and darkened along all but the main roads as the council did not have enough men to remove the anti-Zeppelin covers. The church bells rang out only intermittently, for many of the change-ringers were still in France. Northern Command announced that fireworks would be permitted. But fireworks were hard to come by.

For too many Nottingham folk, in any case, joy was not the emotion that first rose in their hearts that afternoon. An anonymous parent had reminded them in a letter to that morning's papers:

It would be a gracious and kindly action on the part of the general public if, when peace is celebrated, they would modify their gaiety in consideration for the feelings of countless numbers who have been so sadly bereaved and for whom there will be no homecoming family reunion

149

but only the memory of a nameless grave.
I am, sir, etc.,
Bereaved of our only child

Others were apprehensive of what the peace might bring. Two of Nottingham's notable gentry made cautionary speeches. Lord Henry Bentinck told a large gathering in Pennyfoot Street that Nottinghamshire alone had 78,000 men serving in the forces, for whom there awaited few jobs, poor wages and scandalously neglected housing. A few streets away the Duke of Portland announced that there could be no mawkish sentiment towards those who had brought untold horrors upon the world, and that all of them, from the Kaiser downwards, should receive the retribution they deserved. He trusted the government would restrict the flow of undesirable foreigners. Great Britain should not be a dumping-place for those who — he was poised to use strong words — were 'the scum of the Continent'.

At four o'clock, slight rain was dampening the gathering gloom at Nottingham's Midland Station as another damper on excessive excitement pulled into platform two. A full train-load of wounded from the final battle for Arras was lifted out and put on to the waiting ambulances. It was a slow business. Many of the men were desperately ill and the stretcher-bearers were elderly. Nottingham had few able-bodied men left for the home front.

In the narrow front windows of the fifteenth-century Flying Horse Hotel in Nottingham, Percy Toplis sat watching the ambulances go past through the market square. Knots of people waved Union Jacks at them. Lighted shop windows and open curtains illuminated the soggy bunting wrapped around the lamp standards.

But Toplis was not to be depressed. On the contrary, 11 a.m. on 11 November marked the beginning of what he was confident was an extremely successful day for him. As from that moment he felt himself immune from the firing squad. Not that there had ever been any sign of the dullards in the Military Police looking in the army's own records for the whereabouts of their 'most wanted deserter'. For, on his arrival back in England, Toplis had taken the boldest course, gone straight to the army recruiting centre in Nottingham and joined another regiment, the Royal Army Service Corps.

He had been taken to Clipstone Camp, his new depot. It was comfortably near Shirland, a village close to Alfreton in Derbyshire where his mother had just moved, and the duties were hardly onerous. There were hardly any duties at all. The celebration of the Armistice had not been constrained at Clipstone by the solemn sentiments of Nottingham. When the news had arrived — a newsboy with a quire of *Evening Post* specials — Private Toplis had made immediately for his place of duty, the canteen piano.

He knew the favourite tunes, especially 'The Old Hundredth'. But the singing had not lasted long. There were too many men who wanted to be off to girlfriends and families. And there were few enough among the soldiers present who knew anything of Mons and Ypres or Passchendaele and the Somme. There was little sentiment to be wrung from 'the long, long way to Tipperary'. And the pubs were open in Ollerton. Toplis had realized that it was time to prepare for the imperatives of peace. He had gone back to his billet and carefully packed the equipment which was to provide him with a living: one full walking-out uniform of an officer in the Royal Army Service Corps, complete with Mons decoration and a number of chevrons on the sleeve; one chequebook drawn on the London County and Westminster Bank at Beckenham, Kent, originally the property of a certain Lieutenant Copeland Barker of London; and a revolver with twelve cartridges.

Toplis had tested the less violent aspects of his equipment a month before at Hucknall on his way in to a weekend's furlough in Nottingham. He had called in at Frank Tweed's jewellery shop in the High Street and looked at a number of gold bracelet watches. There was a fine Benson for £8 17s. 6d. But as Toplis started to write out one of Lieutenant Copeland's cheques, he sensed that Mr Tweed was becoming uneasy, and that a Mons star might not be a total guarantee of

151

credit-worthiness. With a flourish he scribbled in the sum of £9. 'The extra half a crown is the mark of a gentleman', he cried, and walked out with the watch. A fortnight before that, a bank at Mansfield Woodhouse had fallen for the same style.

Now that the fighting had stopped, Toplis felt he could abandon the army for the time being. In the post-war confusion he could find both security and opportunity in the outside world. The Flying Horse had not been difficult about honouring a cheque on this day of all days, and Toplis saw no reason to do his drinking anywhere else but in its comfortable lounge. As the evening set in, more revellers appeared, determined to overcome the atmosphere of sobriety. A lorry crammed with American soldiers, cheering wildly and flying the Stars and Stripes, tore through the market place. A stray aircraft dropped Verey lights, and parties of girls from the munitions factory marched up and down waving flags and singing. Toplis called for another black beer. As he turned round, two men walked in through the door and strode straight towards him. One was Detective Sergeant Hames, Nottingham Police. The other Toplis recognized immediately as Mr Frank Tweed, jeweller of Hucknall. Temporarily the peace had started badly for Percy Toplis.

For a fortnight, the police attempted to make inquiries into the background of their prisoner. There were two adjournments of the case for further investigations. This only served to encourage Toplis, and the police got everything wrong. His age was given as thirty — ten years too much; his occupation as miner — six years out of date; his army unit as the Royal Army Medical Corps stationed at Salonika.

Toplis, familiar with the ways of the magistrates, concentrated on diversions and sympathy ploys rather than contesting the charges. He told the Nottinghamshire Hall Bench that he had only tried the frauds because his war wounds affected him. When the magistrates proved unmoved, he coolly asked for the return of £7 which had been found on him. Their worships declined and dispatched him to six months' hard labour. The army gave him a dishonourable discharge. It was to be the last time the law would catch up with Percy Toplis — alive.

14

As the spring of 1919 moved into summer, the hopes and expectations of the Armistice sagged into bitterness, confusion and conflict. The great armies which had broken through into Germany the previous autumn had expected to be in Berlin within a week, followed by a brief nibble at the fruits of victory and a quick demobilization, after which it would be 'back to their cats and canaries', good quiet jobs and homes fit for heroes. Six months later, they knew it was not to happen thus.

The truce had locked the armies impatiently in aspic. Germany might refuse the terms. The Allies might need to fight again. Right through the winter of 1918/19 the troops had waited for the peace talks to begin. The food was, if anything, even worse than during the war. There were riots and disturbances. Two companies of the Hampshires refused to parade. One of the ringleaders was taken in. A London Rifle Brigade man reported 'turbulent scenes' when the news came that recruits who had only been with the brigade a month or two were to be demobilized before veterans who had served since 1914. Bitterly, he recorded another Christmas in uniform:

One eighteenth part of a scraggy turkey. No gravy. Beef.
Potatoes. Three and a half ounces of pudding. Unsweet-
ened custard. Three quarters of a fig. One third of a rotten
apple. And paper chains.

The sense of grievance grew when it was rumoured,
correctly, that large batches of troops who had never left
England's shores were being demobilized.

Peace officially came and went with the signing of the
treaty in June 1919. But in that month there were still ten full
divisions in the Rhineland. The streets of Cologne saw British
machine-gun posts, both the German and the British
authorities being in fear of a Red revolution. The troops
stayed on, with prison sentences and heavy punishments to
contain their discontent.

Back home in England there was little comfort. The
miners, as a starred occupation, had been conscripted late
and demobilized early. They returned to the pits in early
1919 to find crippling inflation and a confrontation with the
mine-owners. By July there was an all-out strike in the
Yorkshire coalfield and trouble in Wales and Scotland.
When the rest of the troops did get home, there would be few
jobs, and many of the men returning would be unfit for the
jobs that there were.

Into this confused and tense situation Percy Toplis
emerged from jail in Nottingham. Norman de Courcy Parry,
the chief constable's son, whose path was to cross fatally with
Toplis, recalls this period:

'The country had very quickly become flooded with men
for whom there was no hope of employment, men who had
been wounded, gassed, or shell-shocked, and men who had
never learned any trade at all but the art of killing their fellow
men, men who were accustomed to survive under circumstances of intense hardship and discomfort which civilians
were unable to envisage.

'Intense bitterness and resentment arose between the
returned soldier and those who had remained at home in
lucrative situations, and had even taken their girlfriends.

'The war was forgotten, and to many crime seemed to be the simplest way of making a living. The police were faced with ruthless men, caring for nothing, and extremely experienced in combat as well. There was no way of dealing with those who were out of touch with reality, and those needing just the slightest mental assistance did not receive it. Many had brainstorms, many more could not sleep without a light, and sudden noise, a creaking door, or the crash of something breaking up, might send even a strong man temporarily hysterical. It was a very intense time for parents and wives.'

For Toplis, neither parents nor wives were a consideration — and confusion was his natural element.

So it was that in the summer of 1919 a confident young man of 22 presented himself once again at a recruiting office, this time in London, and re-enlisted in the Royal Army Service Corps as No. 54262 Toplis, Francis Percy. The continued effrontery is incredible. Two hundred and sixty-three men were officially admitted to have been shot for desertion — six of them in that very year, 1919. Yet Toplis, as renowned a deserter as any in the land, got back into the army under his own name. To this day the army have no explanation, and they maintain that they cannot check. The official line is that his wartime papers must have been among those destroyed at a Walworth warehouse during the blitz on London in the Second World War, a blaze that conveniently removed the papers of another figure from the Étaples mutiny, Corporal Wood.

It was not, however, Toplis's intention to require too much from the army. Just food, pay and an occasional bed. In return, he did not intend the army to require too much from him. In this spirit, Driver Toplis, Mechanical Section Royal Army Service Corps, arrived with a draft at the Avonmouth Depot near Bristol in August 1919.

He had not chosen to stay in the service corps by accident. In that frenetic year after the ending of the war the corps had become the mob of the British Army — and Bristol was its Chicago. For the service corps had access to a liquor craved as urgently in Britain as booze was in Prohibition America: petrol. Percy Toplis stepped into the barracks at Avonmouth aware not only that the corps would feed and clothe him, but that it could also provide a handsome living. What he did not know was that the corps already had its Al Capone gang — the Redskins.

Private V. Scott of Heywood, Lancashire, then a young lad of 17, remembers the reign of terror the Redskins maintained inside the barracks:

'We slept on bed boards laid out on trestles with straw mattresses on top. These had to be kept clean and scrubbed. The Redskins just ordered the young ones to do the work for them. If they didn't they were beaten up. These were old soldiers who hadn't taken their discharge after the war and they meant business. One of them always carried a cut-throat razor with him. And he wasn't afraid to use it. In the end it all finished up with a murder. But long before that we were terrified into doing anything they wanted.'

The terror in the barrack room, however, was a mere sideline to the Redskins. Their main objective was the weekly milking from the tanks at Avonmouth Depot of thousands of gallons of petrol which on the black market could fetch double the official price. The Redskins had the system inside Avonmouth camp sewn up. They happily left the young recruits to play around on the huge caterpillar tractors learning to manoeuvre the big guns while they concentrated on the lorries and cars. There was a Redskin on every shift at the 'oil well', checking out each driver from the pumps. Every driver had to sign for a full tank of petrol and take half a tank. There were Redskins in the Quartermaster's Office checking and approving the sheets, there were Redskins on the gates, and Redskin drivers to take full loads of petrol out to the market.

By the time Toplis arrived, the Redskin leader, Corporal Harry Pearson, had the organization running with exemplary smoothness, except for that perennial bane of the entrepreneur: distribution. There was an immediate treaty. According to Private Scott, the Redskins knew of Toplis, some of them having been at Étaples. Certainly they recognized a fearsome opponent or a powerful ally — and settled for peace. Toplis's toughness was known and proven. By late 1919, his patina of elegant and confident trickster was lacquered beyond fear of flaking on to four years of war experience.

Toplis set about organizing the transport owners of Bristol. As long as they paid cash on the nail they were guaranteed a regular delivery of army petrol at whatever time was most convenient to avoid the eyes of prying employees or the attentions of the constabulary. Toplis negotiated in the most relaxed style, meeting at the old Guildhall pub in Bristol, or even journeying to the Assembly Rooms at Bath if there was a particularly handsome deal on the horizon. There was never any mention of the problem of the law, or hint of the presence of the Redskin heavies.

But the alliance with the Redskins was strictly business. Back at the barracks, Toplis remained aloof and as lordly as a loafer in St James's. Young Scott was employed at 2s. 6d. a week to scrub the Toplis bed board. There was 6d. here or 1s. there to spare Percy the other minor impositions of army life.

For three months the operation flowed on without a ripple. Then, in October 1919, the army intervened in its usual capricious fashion. A draft notice arrived ordering Scott, Toplis and the Redskins to Bulford Camp on Salisbury Plain. There was talk of protest, even desertion, but Toplis airily assured them that there would be ample, even greater, opportunities in the sprawling morass of the Royal Army Service Corps' biggest base. And so it was to prove.

Bulford was, indeed, to provide another revolving stage for the display of Toplis's exotic talents: exploiting the army, entertaining the troops, painting London red, seducing the ladies, becoming involved in a murder and, finally, sparking off the fatal, fascinated manhunt which was to rivet the attention of British newspaper readers for more than six weeks before its climax on the lonely road in Cumberland.

157

Bulford more than lived up to Percy's expectations. As Private John Anderson of Felling-on-Tyne recalls:

'It was a shambles. People were joining up in their thousands. And war veterans were trying to get out in their thousands. No one knew what anyone was doing. The new recruits hadn't been kitted out or sorted into companies. The old soldiers went round in civilian clothes, it was chaos. The young lads in off the street like me were starving. They had to put military police on the dining halls to stop us coming round for second helpings. The rackets were enormous. The cooks were selling off food to people in Salisbury, often before it even got delivered to the camp. And of course it was the biggest driving school. There were stacks of lorries and stacks of petrol.'

Toplis and the Redskins settled in. There were not so many transport firms around, but Toplis soon homed in on the readiest of markets. The taxi drivers of Winchester, Salisbury, even Southampton, were only too eager to keep their faltering trade topped up with army petrol. Rumour had it that the contact man was a certain Sidney Spicer, who drove a cab in Salisbury. Certainly his trade, illicit or not, was to prove within the year abruptly fatal for himself and for Toplis.

In the meantime, with a comfortable income assured, Toplis set about enjoying himself. The weekends, from Thursday to Tuesday, were reserved for a Burlington Bertie life in the metropolis. The press was later to discover his tracks at the Savoy and Ascot, his buying shoes in Pall Mall and suits in Savile Row, his recounting, as 'Captain Williams', exploits at Hill 60, his philandering with the daughters of the aristocracy and compromising young ladies in teashops. But, for a couple of days midweek, with Thursday's pay parade in view, it was pleasant enough to wander around impressing the lads back at Bulford.

His young friend, 19-year-old Private Harry Fallows, built up an awed picture of Toplis's army life. It was rare to see Percy in the same uniform twice running. He had an endless supply of badges, from RAF to Army Remount. He appeared sometimes as a private soldier, sometimes as a sergeant-major, often as an officer, and then invariably adorned with his gold-rimmed monocle. One memorable day, Fallows says, he appeared in the camp in the uniform of a full colonel:

'He walked out of the hut and down towards the canteen. He told me to follow a few yards behind. The young blokes just melted out of the way. Anyone who got trapped in his path brought off a mighty salute because officers weren't seen much round there. But then, as we got near the canteen hut, a bunch of old hands came out. They saw him, but it was against their principles to salute anyone. Percy wasn't having that. He could put on this real toff gentleman's voice. And he roared out: "Soldier, don't you know the rules of this Army. Let's see your arm up there. And again. Faster, or I'll damn well shoot it off for you." And at that, he whipped this Webley 6 revolver out of his holster and fired off three shots. Just like that. One, two, three. The soldiers just hit the ground and stayed there. When they looked up "Colonel" Toplis was doubled up with laughter, shouting: "Just where you belong, Thomas. Just where you belong." They were chaps he knew, you see. He'd fired all right, but the bullets had gone in the ground. He just told the lads to come down and have a drink with him.

'For all that, he had too much of that revolver in the camp. He had a lot to say about it. He kept talking about doing this and that. In the end we took no notice. It was well known in the camp that he was a deserter. He had a set of proper discharge papers. But once, when I was a temporary clerk in the company office, I copied out a confidential document which said he was a deserter and gave it to him.'

Clearly the army knew that it had taken the viper back into its bosom. But authority did nothing. By Christmas, according to Fallows, Toplis rarely bothered to show up at the camp at all. He would appear on Wednesday evening in time for Thursday's pay parade, and then vanish again. Occasionally he would while away a few hours making out his own leave passes and handing them to the soldiers.

In this war of nerves the army seemed afraid to lift a finger.

159

The embarrassments of Toplis's past army life were daily compounded by new audacities, but the present indignities were puny compared with the revelations which might have accompanied a public court martial. Finally it was Toplis who tired of the pantomime. On Boxing Night, Fallows was on duty as orderly in the depot vehicle office when a Sunbeam car appeared outside the window. Fallows peered out and thought he recognized Percy at the wheel. As the car reached the gate the sentry challenged it. The car stopped with the engine running, the driver produced a chit, the sentry saluted — and the car was on its way. Toplis was opting out of the Royal Army Service Corps for the time being, with the bonus of the Sunbeam car, property of the War Office, value £100.

It was the car that finally outraged the army. Its description, and that of its driver, were circulated quickly as Toplis set off across Salisbury Plain, intent on spending New Year with a lady of his acquaintance in Bath. For the purposes of this particular romance he was a company sergeant-major.

The afternoon of 27 December found him walking out in the full-dress uniform of his rank with Miss Evelyn Shipton, the daughter of a greengrocer in the town. It was still a bright clear day as he parked the Sunbeam outside the Pump Rooms and helped Miss Shipton out. Over the road was a small café of sentimental memory to the couple. They had often taken tea there when Toplis had been on business visits from Bristol. The car had put Miss Shipton in an affectionate mood. Clearly her young hero had been doing well. Despite a little residual pique at his three-month absence, she let his hand rest on her knee as the waitress arrived with the cakes. There had been a moment of indiscretion, fortunately with no dire results, the night Percy had left for Bulford. She was determined not to repeat it, at least not so soon. Yet Percy was not only attractive, but also persuasive. Miss Shipton glanced out at the car. A little trip to the country perhaps. 'People seem to admire your car,' she said. Percy looked up to see two military policemen surveying the front of the Sunbeam. They turned and began to walk across the road. Swiftly Toplis got up and made for the door. Coolly he held it open while the two Red Caps walked in and went over to speak to the waitress. He was round the corner and running before he heard the sounds of pursuit. By the time he got to the Great Western Railway Station there was no sign of the chase and a train was in for Bristol, Exeter and Plymouth. Thankfully he settled back in a third-class carriage. The train was full of soldiers. There were one or two military policemen. But they would not lightly tangle with a company sergeant-major.

Down at Bristol Temple Meads station, however, was a Red Cap with no such scruples. Corporal Arthur Rayment, boxer and veteran of Étaples and the Western Front, had had a busy Christmas. A whole battalion of Irish troops bound reluctantly for India had simply got off the train at Temple Meads, officers and all, and declined to continue. Rayment had spent a few hours rounding them up from the pubs of Bristol, ending up with their captain, dead drunk in a hotel bedroom. On Christmas Eve, Rayment had been attacked by a huge wild Canadian brandishing a cut-throat razor. Rayment had felled him with a punch of knuckle-duster force, but only after getting a fair beating himself. The message that now came down the line was scarcely welcome.

'Please detain and hold passenger on 4.35 Bath/Bristol train. Wearing uniform of Company Sergeant-Major. May be armed. Name Francis Percy Toplis. Description: Medium height, reddish hair. Age 22. Looks older.'

Rayment took three colleagues and went across to Platform No. 4. Troops piled off the train, but there was no sign of the distinctive sleeve of a company sergeant-major. Rayment warned the guard to hold the train and boarded the end carriage. He was prepared for a fight. It seemed unlikely that his man would use a gun in a crowded train. Slowly he edged down the train over the mêlée of kit-bags into the second coach. At the far end a company sergeant-major was coming out of the lavatory. Instinctively, Toplis decided to bluff it out.

'What the hell do you mean, Corporal? I warn you, I'm not used to being approached in this way. If you'll just get out of the way I can get back to my seat.'

161

Rayment, a big man, gripped him by the arm. 'I'm sorry, I have written orders to take you off this train for questioning.' Quietly enough Toplis capitulated. This was neither the time nor the place for force. The policemen searched him and removed the Webley. Chatting cheerfully, Toplis was taken back to the police post.

In the truculent array of drunks, trouble-makers and victims of fights that Christmas of 1919, Toplis, the absentee, seemed hardly to need special watching. In any case, the cells were full. Rayment himself had arrested seventeen people that day. He was happy enough to fill in Form 13252 and see Toplis packed off to the overspill guard-room down the river at Shirehampton Remount Depot, a stone's throw from old familiar territory at Avonmouth.

For Toplis, survivor of the death cell at Étaples, who had masqueraded his way back to England from Boulogne under the noses of Secret Service agents, Shirehampton was a push-over. The second night he joined casually in a game of pontoon with his guards. It was a game he had learnt in a hard school with the Aussies at Étaples. He was winning comfortably. The guards were boys with no idea when to risk a fifth card or how to hide a good banker's hand. Towards midnight, one left to check the log. When he came back, it was to find his colleague staring at his own pistol in Toplis's hands. A simple bit of pick-pocketing had sufficed. Toplis locked them both in his own cell and walked out of the depot. Nerve, confidence and experience had stood him in good stead once again. He was free to face the arrival of the New Year of 1920 in jovial mood. It was to be his last, since he was to die by June.

Toplis did not at that moment, however, wish to desert His Majesty's Services altogether. The wages and the accommodation were not to be scoffed at in such troubled times. By January he was enrolled in the Royal Air Force. Even now, more than fifty years on, the RAF are less than keen to admit any responsibility for a man who had taken their more senior service for a helter-skelter ride through five years of war and peace. He was enlisted as Aircraftman Francis

162

Percy Toplis. They paid him. Nothing else is forthcoming.

In all the colourful Toplis story of 1920, the army kept a low profile, but the RAF stayed invisible. The last chapter in the chronicle of Percy Toplis, deserter, hero, confidence trickster, ladies' man, mutineer, Bolshevik, escape artist, and gentleman of St James's, began with a crime Toplis had never before been embroiled in: murder.

On the balmy morning of Sunday, 25 April, Sidney Spicer, the young Salisbury taxi driver, was found shot in the head under a hedge at Thruxton Down, near Andover, in Hampshire. The body had been dragged for forty yards across the road over the bank and into the hedge. There were blood marks on the tarmac. The local police acted quickly. They issued this description of the man they wanted for the murder:

Name: Private Percy Toplis, Regimental number EMT 54262 RASC, enlisted August 1919, deserted December 1919, of smart appearance, affects a gold monocle. Age 34 or 35, sometimes has ginger moustache, cut à la Charlie Chaplin.

Superintendent Cox of the Hampshire Police was unforthcoming about the evidence against Toplis, but to his thinking it was sufficient to launch the most intense and dramatic post-war manhunt. For six weeks the hunted man ranged the length of Britain, flaunted himself, then melted away; tantalized the newspaper-reading public with exploit after exploit, before, like Pearl White herself, invariably escaping in the nick of time.

Within three days of the murder, Superintendent Cox arrested Toplis's friend, Private Harry Fallows, and charged him with harbouring and maintaining Toplis. The same day the inquest on Sidney Spicer opened in the rather original setting of a barn at Thruxton Down, with grain heaped on the floor, harness hanging from old beams under a ceiling concealed with cobwebs. Members of the nine-man jury, as well as the Deputy Coroner, Captain J. T. P. Clarke, sat on

163

bags of chaff. The coroner opened by declaring proudly: 'This court has got one piece of evidence that is not available in any other court, and that is the body of the deceased man.' And sure enough there the body was, in an open box outside the barn door. The jury trooped out for a look.

Coroner Clarke sought to explain the emotive choice of a barn, yards away from the spot where the body had been found. From his seat on the chaff bag, above him a horse saddle hanging on the wall, he said, 'The circumstances of the case are probably known to all of you better than me. It is one of those tragedies that occurs in an out of the way part of Hampshire and gives it a world-wide interest. That reason has induced me to adjourn from the small room in the farmhouse to this barn. The room that we were offered was small and would have been uncomfortably crowded.'

The inquest was then adjourned with only evidence of identification. By the time it was resumed in more easeful circumstances more than a month later at Shipton School, a local magistrates' court had started proceedings against Private Fallows on the charge of harbouring.

The first thing that their worships heard from a Mr Sims, acting for the public prosecutor, was that the army was washing its hands of Toplis as fast as possible. He was disowned and dumped on the RAF as their problem. Mr Sims said, 'There can be no doubt at all that the person who inflicted that wound on Spicer was an ex-soldier named Toplis, a deserter from the RAF at the time, masquerading as a quartermaster-sergeant.'

Although it was Private Fallows who was on trial, the story of Toplis and the fateful weekend dominated the proceedings. Slowly the story, or at least a version of the story, began to emerge.

Despite the little adventure with the army's Sunbeam car, and the inconvenience in Bath and Bristol, Toplis had not deserted his business interests at Bulford Camp entirely. Harry Fallows reported that his friend Percy had shown up several times for a meal and a chat at the cookhouse. He had strolled about the camp, saying that he was a civilian

164

attached to the Air Force Commission in London. There were discussions with the Redskins about the petrol racket. The police, military and civilian, were causing no difficulties, but some of the taxi firms were cutting up rough about the price and threatening to spill the story to the authorities. Through March and April no action seemed necessary, and Toplis cheerfully called in on Fallows from time to time in the company mess at No. 2 Depot, had a bite to eat and then faded away back to London.

On the Saturday afternoon of 24 April, Fallows was asleep on his bunk at Bulford when a corporal came into the hut and said: 'A sergeant-major wishes to see you.' Fallows went out down the mile-long winding hill from the camp towards the Rose and Crown. There was Sergeant-Major Toplis playing the piano alone in the Cromwell Institute, picking out his favourite tune — 'Let the Great Big World Keep Turning'.

Toplis stopped and turned to Fallows: 'Do you fancy a stroll?'

They had only gone a few paces when a Red Cap sergeant stopped them and asked Fallows if he had a pass. Toplis, as usual, was immune because of his uniform, but they both turned back. Near the Bulford railway siding Toplis put his coat down and they sat down in the sun. A small dog came bounding up and they romped with it for a few minutes. But Toplis was restless. Shortly he said he would come back at three o'clock on Sunday afternoon to give Fallows a ride in a landaulette car which he had bought. He put his monocle in his eye, said good-bye and turned to go towards Bulford Station. For a moment he paused: 'Still got the old friend.' And he dropped six bullets out of the chambers of a Mark 6 Webley revolver.

'You're a fool to carry a thing like that about in England,' said Fallows.

'Well, I'm going to Ireland soon. You can shoot on sight there.' And he was on his way.

That small exchange was to seal Toplis's fate.

It was only a few hours later, however, at eleven o'clock

that same Saturday night, according to Harry Fallows, that Toplis came back to Bulford:

'He knocked at the door of the cookhouse. I thought it was the provost sergeant and opened the door, but it was Toplis, and he said, "For God's sake give me a drink. I feel as parched as hell." I gave him a drink of tea and he said if I didn't go on the joy-ride to Tidworth right then, I should not be able to have one at all as he had some business on. He borrowed a towel to wipe his hands, but he didn't wash.

'Instead of starting the car, Toplis gave it a push down the hill towards the railway siding, jumped in and threw the clutch in. I asked him why he did it that way. He said he didn't want everybody poking about.

'At North Tidworth he changed hats with me. When I was picking his up from behind the seat, I found his revolver. It was still loaded in all six chambers. When we got to Savernake Forest we had a bit of sleep. But first he took some clothes out of the front of the car, took them about twenty yards away, put some petrol on them and burnt them. He said they were oily rags. It was no use leaving them in the car and he wanted to warm his hands.' At Cirencester the car stopped dead out of petrol. Toplis bought a tin. By ten o'clock on Sunday morning, while Superintendent Cox was viewing the body on Thruxton Down, the two motorists had reached Gloucester and the car had broken down. They had it repaired. But it was not Toplis's day. On the way down through the Forest of Dean he hit a cow and it took an hour to straighten out the bumper and mudguard so that it was nearly seven in the evening before they reached Swansea. With every hour that passed the beautiful Darracq car was becoming a more conspicuous and dangerous liability.

They stayed at the Grosvenor Hotel, Fallows recollects, Toplis with his revolver beside his bed:

'We slept until ten o'clock. He told me then to buck up. I wasn't moving quick enough. We had breakfast. He went into a barber's shop and had a shave, and left me alone. I met him coming out of a garage down the street with the car. He shouted for me to jump in and said, "That man won't buy the car, he thinks I've stolen it." There was a policeman at the bottom of the hill and Toplis said: "He's watching us. You get out here." He borrowed my spectacles. I walked round and met him at the bottom of the road. Toplis was tense. "You had better get back to Bulford quickly." '

He thrust a pound in Fallows's hand and gave him back his own cap. Fallows shook hands with Toplis for the last time and caught the train to Salisbury. Toplis set off for familiar territory, across the River Severn to Bristol.

Back at Bulford there was uproar, as Private Jack Anderson remembers:

'Everybody was ordered out of their huts by the military police and we all had to stand while they got underneath the huts and searched. We had a chap apparently in our lot that looked very much like him. They took him away and gave him a right going over before he could prove where he had been. The whole camp was sealed off and it was hours before we were allowed back in our billets. There was no going to the canteen. Nothing. Even to us new recruits, Toplis was a well-known figure at the camp. He was a well-spoken chap and we all knew he went off to London and posed as an admiral or something. But that day no one seemed to have anything to say to the police.'

Meanwhile Superintendent Cox was trying to work out a timetable of murder. He had some witnesses. Private Jack Holdrick at the RASC's Embarkation Depot at Southampton Docks had come forward to say he had seen Toplis on the Saturday afternoon, also at about half past two, near the Clock House in Southampton High Street. According to Holdrick, he asked Toplis what he was doing. 'He said he had had his ticket from the RASC and was in the Air Force. Toplis said: "You know the car missing from Bulford on Boxing Night? It was me. I sold it in Cirencester for £100. I am going to Bulford to get another one. If I can't get it by fair means I shall do it with this." '

Holdrick then told the police that Toplis had produced a Webley service revolver from his back trouser pocket, and confirmed he was wearing a sergeant-major's crown on his arm and RAF khaki. Yet this melodramatic and hardly characteristic encounter amid the shopping crowds at Southampton apparently took place at the same time as, according to Fallows, Toplis was playing the piano to himself twenty-five miles away in the Cromwell Institute at Bulford.

Another RASC man, Driver Arthur Sellwood, told the police he left Salisbury at about nine o'clock on Saturday evening in Sidney Spicer's taxi. When they arrived near Amesbury railway bridge on the journey to Bulford they had to fill up. Just then a man came out of the hedge near-by, walked to the driver and asked him to take him to Andover. Spicer said he was going the other way, but would call for him on the way back if he wanted. Sellwood said the stranger had a British Warm coat with a sergeant-major's crown on the sleeve.

Superintendent Cox then tried out the complicated journey this evidence suggested: from Amesbury railway bridge through to the Rose and Crown at Bulford where the car had been seen to turn round; back to Amesbury to pick up the stranger; then on via Andover to the fatal spot at Thruxton Hill; and back to Bulford and No. 2 Company Depot by eleven o'clock in time to meet Fallows. Sixteen miles: it was possible. Indeed, the story was good enough for the Andover coroner. People did not usually parade with revolvers and draw them on every conceivable occasion, he told the inquest jury. Toplis had been seen in the same uniform as that worn by the mysterious stranger at Amesbury. Captain Clarke admitted that there seemed to be a little discrepancy about time, but not too much notice should be taken of that. People did not know what they were doing every minute of the day. The jury was absent for about fifteen minutes. Returning to court, the foreman said they were agreed that Spicer had met his death as a result of gunshot wounds. And they returned a verdict of 'wilful murder' against Percy Toplis. If caught, he would now certainly be hanged.

The inquest was the first in modern times to declare a man guilty of murder in his absence. At this distance it seems by no means certain that Toplis really was the killer. The case was far from conclusive, based, as it was, largely on a man who had turned King's Evidence, Private Fallows.

There had been no sign of blood on Toplis. His revolver was still fully loaded when Fallows found it. Toplis was apparently in two places at once, twenty-five miles apart, at 2.30 on the day of the murder. The motive of murdering to joy-ride in a car is a thin one indeed. But, from that moment, Toplis stood no chance. He was a condemned and convicted murderer who would never have been able to prove his innocence. He had been publicly branded as an outlaw.

The hue and cry was now in earnest. The discrepancies, along with the unchallenged assertion of the inquest, were swept aside in the frenetic hunt for 'The Most Dangerous Man in Britain'. Five days before, at the magistrates' court, Private Fallows had been cleared completely of the charges against him.

During the six weeks he was on the run, sightings of Toplis were reported from 107 different places throughout Britain. Every newspaper and every police station carried photographs and descriptions of the murderer with the monocle. Almost each day there were spurious sightings and false arrests. In the Welsh mountains, children joined police in the search. In Wiltshire, a man who looked like Toplis was beaten up by villagers before he could be rescued by police. One story ended in tragedy: a sad epitaph on the England of 1920 and the excited passions that the hunt for Toplis aroused. It concerned another man whom the public had mistaken for Toplis and enthusiastically hunted down. Alongside a report headlined 'Toplis Still at Large', the *Andover Advertiser* carried this account of the affair on 14 May 1920:

The astounding story of Private Coop of the 9th Lancers had a dramatic ending on Friday morning when Coop was found dead in a cell at the Lancers guardroom at

169

Tidworth, having hung himself with a strip of canvas torn from the top of his trousers.

A hardened deserter, Coop escaped from the guard-room two days before the tragedy. He reached a cottage at Collingbourne and asked for some clothes. But the people at the cottage thought he was Toplis and chased him off. He seized a bike and made towards Burbage. By now a crowd were chasing him, but he kept them off with vicious cuts from a stick until he lost control on a steep hill and police who were following in a car grabbed him. When the regimental police came to get him, he assaulted his escort, seized the district nurse's bike, and set off again. There was a chase over fields until police finally surrounded him.

At the inquest at Tidworth Major Kemple O.B.E. said Coop had been in the Lancers since 1908 and had gone right through the war. Private Wild said he had seen Coop trying to hang himself in the cell with a scarf. He cut him down. He had to go in five times to take stuff from him. Coop had then asked to see the MO saying he was suffering from VD. Captain Rupert Hicks RAMC said he had found no evidence of VD and sent him back to the guardroom.

Recalled, Private Wild spoke of the following curiously worded message written on the wall of the dead man's cell in letters a foot high: Dear Jess and wife and mother and dad. I am being murdered. Jess take my body home. Goodbye all.

Major Kemple intimated that although the deceased was probably under the delusion he would be shot for desertion, the adjutant had personally assured him that this was not to be so.

This news story was not untypical of its time. Justice was a haphazard commodity, and the story bears out de Courcy Parry's observations about the widespread untreated madness caused by the war.

Meanwhile Toplis, more rational, was keeping a terse diary.

April 19: Bulford.

April 25: Entry erased.

May 21: [the day of Fallows's acquittal on the charge of harbouring Toplis] Harry released.

May 26: [The day he read about the Spicer inquest verdict of his own guilt] La verdict. Rotten.

There was only one personal note. It was back on 4 April: 'Freshford with Dorothy'. In all the lurid speculation which was to follow, Dorothy was to remain a mystery.

15

When 'General' Toplis reached the remote Banffshire Highlands in Scotland on Tuesday, 1 June 1920, the strong probability is that he felt his road was winding uphill all the way, and certainly, in a strictly physical sense, he was right. Toplis was now in the area of the superlative: the highest, the loneliest and the loveliest. The sight that greeted him was not all that much different from the one that had so impressed another general, George Wade, when he first arrived to civilize the Highlanders after the Jacobite Rebellion of 1715.

One of General Wade's main tasks two hundred years previously had been to provide adequate roads, but although it was named the Old Military Road, Wade had not given over-much attention to the one on which Toplis walked, and sometimes cycled, towards Upper Donside on that hot summer day. He was travelling in a south-easterly direction from Grantown-on-Spey, and just south of Tomintoul the road became a rough, narrow track over moors and mountains, and occasionally, wide expanses of desolation, but the overall impression was one of wild, intense beauty.

He dismounted and walked beside his bicycle, wearying feet negotiating the steep slopes of the mountainous area

172

known as the Lecht. Its highest point, 3,843 feet up, looked down on the Rivers Don and Dee, the Gairn and the Avon, all in close proximity, each competing with the other in sheer magnificence and a wealth of boundless mountain scenery.

In a hollow to the south side of the Don was Gorgarff Castle, a former stronghold of the English in the far, upland country where countless pure, white streams cascaded down the mountain-sides to the rivers below. This castle had been acquired by the government after the Jacobite risings, and it was from here that government troops had continued attempting to cow the proud Highlanders into subjection long after the main battles had ceased.

That afternoon the outlawed Toplis acquired his own little piece of mountain property: the Lecht Shooting Lodge. By midnight, it was to prove an appropriate name. The bicycle which he propped against the timbered wall of the shooting lodge was to figure in subsequent police descriptions thus:

Twenty six inch black enamelled frame with red and yellow lines (faint) 28 inch wheels, two lever brakes, rims and handlebars plated but rusty, black celluloid handle grips, left one minus end, small sized saddle marked C83. Manufactured by Lycett Saddle Co. Ltd., Birmingham, carrier attached with screw driver, 'Edinburgh' tyre on front wheel, well worn. Rear tyre recently repaired. Tool bag with celluloid name plate, but no name.

[The rider of the bicycle] Gave the name, George Williams, and his age as 30 years (looks younger) said he was American and that he was demobilised from Army some time ago, had American accent, about 5 feet 8 inches in height, slender built, small eyes, hair variously described as sandy, reddish fair, auburn, clean shaven, ruddy complexion, longish thin face.

Dressed in khaki trousers, puttees, light grey jacket and greenish or greyish felt Trilby type hat, carried white canvas bag, probably a kit bag.

Toplis, now alias Williams, had exercised his considerable

173

charm effectively when peddling pennilessly through Tomintoul at 4 p.m. that afternoon. He had the punctured rear tyre repaired at a cycle shop, and when charged 2s., agitatedly searched through his pockets before announcing that he had lost £1. He then persuaded the repair man to lend him 5s., promising that he would pay the fee and repay the loan next day. With the 5s. he bought some bread and some milk which he stuffed into his kitbag.

The three-roomed, partially furnished shooting lodge was unoccupied, and Toplis entered by forcing open a window catch with his pocket knife. His luck was still holding. Across the length of Britain a string of witnesses were recalling more or less ruefully encounters with the country's 'most wanted man'. Back in Blaina, a mountainous district in Monmouthshire, police were assisting villagers in remembering a night three weeks before.

On 12 May, 1920, a prayer meeting was in progress at the tiny Salem Baptist Chapel, Blaina, when a light-haired stranger, wearing a muffler and carrying a trilby hat, tiptoed into the back pew and sat himself down between two deacons. He was handed a hymn book and got to his feet to join enthusiastically in the chorus:

'Bread of heaven,
Bread of heaven,
Feed me till I want no more.'

The timbre of his voice rang out above, but did not drown, the practised tones of the twenty worshippers in front of him, and they kept stealing backward glances to catch a glimpse of the new man in their midst. When the service finished fifteen minutes later, most of the congregation gathered round the dirty-faced young visitor, who apologetically explained that he was destitute and that he had walked from London where he frequently attended mission services in the Whitechapel area.

He was on his way to Scotland where he had been promised paid work in a Glasgow mission hall. Touched by his

174

diffident tale, the worshippers volunteered a collection to help him on his way. Coins to the value of 7s. went into the upturned hat. When the police called at the chapel later, a member of the congregation remembered, 'Now you come to mention it, I thought the dirt on his face was faked. He must have fairly plastered it on. But the strangest thing I noticed was that as he was leaving he took a monocle from his pocket and put it to his eye.'

And at London's Victoria Station, a railway detective had spotted the ubiquitous monocle adorning a young gentleman about to go through the barrier for the night Newhaven-Dieppe boat-train. 'Excuse me, sir,' he had accosted him. The man had pocketed the monocle and fled out through the station, dodging the taxi-cabs and away up towards Parliament Square. As an aid to bicycle riding in Scotland, however, Toplis had deemed monocle-wearing a little excessive.

And in the privacy of the shooting lodge from which the rich set forth in season to comb the near-by grouse moors and deerland, such affectations were superfluous. Toplis settled down to sleep away the rest of the first day of June. The chill of the Highland night wakened him at about 9 in the evening in a small room dominated by a large, open fireplace. He had been sleeping on a large, thick tartan rug in front of the empty fire, because, as he had found, the lodge did not have a bed.

The furniture, though sparse, was of grand design, including three George II walnut armchairs and a Louis XVI giltwood writing table. Toplis smashed the chairs on the stone floor, threw the pieces into the fireplace, and followed them up with the writing-table drawer. He then lit his distinguished wood fire and, undressing to his khaki trousers and puttees, flopped down again on the hearth rug. The expensive wood smoke gave off a luxurious aroma as it drifted up the wide chimney into the cold night mountain air.

A Badnafrave farmer, John Grant, saw that column of smoke as he walked home after a hard day shearing sheep on Upper Donside. Grant knew the lodge was supposed to be unoccupied in the laird's absence. The smoke meant only one thing — trespass of the master's property. Without hesitation he walked past his house and two miles along the mountain road to the Altachbeg home of the laird's gamekeeper, John Mackenzie. The two men then walked a further two miles to fetch the only policeman in this entire Highland area, Constable George Greig of Tomintoul. All three then walked back to the shooting lodge, arriving there in the dark at midnight. They found the door locked and the gamekeeper let them in with his key.

The partly dressed Toplis slept on before his expensive fire, a candle fluttering fitfully beside him on the floor. Constable Greig prodded him awake with his boot. Toplis, flat on his back and snoring loudly, was shaken and startled when he looked up at the three figures towering above him. But, with supreme mental effort, he concealed his sense of shock and went on the attack.

'What the hell are you doing here?' he demanded.

Greig, a solid, slow-thinking Highland bobby, was thrown by the audacity of the question. It did not occur to him to retort that that was precisely what he wanted to know about Toplis.

'I apologize for disturbing you, sir. But you'll understand the laird's away. And you appear to be an unauthorized visitor. Can I ask you for your name and address?'

Immediately Toplis realized that his questioner had to be one of the few policemen left in Britain unable to recognize him from the photographs and detailed descriptions littering the land. Or maybe he had reached this remote part ahead of the hue and cry. Or again, maybe it was simply that the candlelight was too meagre for features to be distinguished.

Whatever the reason or reasons, Toplis blessed his luck and decided to go on bluffing. He got up and started to dress. As he put on his shirt, jacket and hat, he assumed an American accent to reply, 'My name is Williams, George Williams.' Then he saw Greig looking at his khaki trousers and puttees and explained, 'I've just come out of the army and I'm in the middle of a hitch-hiking holiday, so if you don't mind I'll be on my way now.'

176

Mackenzie, who had been looking round the room, suddenly whispered to Greig, 'The furniture. He's burned the furniture.'

At last the ponderous Greig had something hard to go on. The visitor had committed a crime, a recognizable, positive crime. Meanwhile Toplis had been manoeuvring himself between the three men and the open door as he stuffed his shaving gear into his kitbag. He pulled the trilby hard down over his eyes and started to back towards the door. Greig moved in his direction, and began to say, 'I'll have to ask you to accompany me ...'

He did not finish the sentence. The hand which had been depositing the shaving gear swiftly re-emerged from the kitbag clasping a gun. His first shot got the policeman in the neck, and he fell to the floor on top of the candle, blood from the wound trickling on to the rug. But before Greig's falling body had snuffed out the candle, Toplis had shot Grant in the belly.

Still without uttering, and now shooting blindly in the dark, Toplis aimed a third shot at where the gamekeeper had been standing. But he missed Mackenzie, who had thrown himself flat on his face on the floor. Toplis rushed out into the blackness, leaped on his cycle and, as he pedalled furiously down the mountain track, the prone Mackenzie could hear him loudly singing the popular wartime song:

> 'Good-byee,
> Don't sigh-ee,
> Wipe the tear, baby dear, from your eye-ee.' '

Toplis had known for some time, as he noted in his diary, that he was doomed and would face the gallows if he was ever caught — knowledge which had finally unhinged his mind.

Mackenzie waited until the sound of the singing had stopped echoing between the mountain peaks, saw that his friends were both unconscious and bleeding badly, got up and started running madly to Tomintoul for assistance. After

177

he had gone, Greig and Grant both regained consciousness, one lying half across the other, the blood of each staining the floor. They dragged themselves to their feet and, holding each other up, stumbled through the darkness down the stony, one-and-a-half-mile pathway to the village of Blairnamarrow. On the doorstep of Dr Black they collapsed again, unconscious.

Next day, Greig and Grant reached the Royal Infirmary, Aberdeen, and the start of a slow recovery, just as Toplis was being given a lift into the same city in a local minister's car. He had sold the bicycle at Strathdon for £1 and hitch-hiked the rest of the way to Aberdeen. The parson remembered his passenger as a man with little to say, a man who carried a kitbag and wore a monocle.

16

Toplis was broke, but he knew that if he could get to Carlisle he would be assured of free board and lodging at the regimental depot. At Aberdeen Station he bought a cup of tea and a platform ticket, two essentials to sustain him on the long journey away from the centre of the manhunt. The train for Carlisle had separate compartments, and Toplis decided it was safer to hide himself away behind ·the boxes of kippers in the guard's van. The cover was poor, and the train had hardly moved out of the station before the guard detected him. For the last time in his life, Toplis's luck held. The guard, Mr James Murray of Southport, felt sorry for him, took out some sandwiches from his snap box and shared them out. Through the long night run down to the Borders, they drank tea and reminisced about the war years. Two days later, Mr Murray realized who his companion had been when he saw the account of Toplis's death and his picture in the newspapers. But he felt unable until now to tell the story of the man for whom he had breached railway regulations.

The net was about to close in on the mutineer, and this time there would be no scope for wriggling free. As Toplis walked down that road to Plumpton and the fatal ambush, the authorities in London were determined that he would ridicule and threaten them no longer. Consultations at the highest level had approved the issuing of firearms. Only an inquest could inquire whether the authorities had also approved orders to kill. Certainly when he reached Plumpton Church on the evening of 6 June 1920, Toplis was given no chance and no quarter. The police made no attempt to question him or arrest him, even though they had the advantage of surprise. He was simply shot at once.

Two hundred yards away from the spot where Percy Toplis slumped, bleeding to death in Inspector Ritchie's arms, there is a roadside memorial. The sign reads:

Do or Die. Here Constable Joseph Byrnes fell on the night of October 29, 1885, shot by three burglars whom he single-handedly endeavoured to arrest.

Constable Byers had been the uncle of Constable Fulton, one of the three officers who ambushed Toplis, and the one whose life Toplis had spared in the confrontation in High Hesket churchyard earlier in the day. Maybe when the Cumberland Police opted to take no chances on an evening thirty-five years later, they remembered the homily. Perhaps it provided the personal justification for ruthlessly carrying out orders which had come from higher authority than their own chief constable. For although Toplis's record was considered dark and deplorable, it seems unlikely that the Cumberland Police would have shot him down quite so callously unless they had been encouraged not to exercise too much care over bringing him in alive. The chief constable, de Courcy Parry, whose second son had been killed in the war, was a compassionate police officer and the shooting was completely out of character.

Mr de Courcy Parry was, of course, unaware that the outlaw might have shot his son, but he presumably did know that he had refrained from shooting Constable Fulton. And it is hard to believe that it mattered not at all to the police on the spot that the man with the monocle should have twice that day refrained from killing one of their associates in circumstances in which he might well have been expected to be remorseless.

As the gentlemen of the nation's press rolled northwards in the hospitable care of the London, Midland and Scottish Railway, some of their editors, notably C. P. Scott of the *Manchester Guardian*, were already formulating misgivings and raising questions about this unprecedented outburst of frontier justice.

Was it necessary to kill a man who had never been charged with violent crime, and who had shown restraint that very day?

Were the police officers entitled to disguise themselves and to come out, guns blazing, without warning?

Could they not have shot merely to incapacitate?

On whose orders were they operating?

Who actually fired the fatal shot?

Where had the guns come from?

What was young de Courcy Parry's role?

The Cumberland Police did not need the newspapers to remind them that these could be somewhat awkward questions. On the Monday afternoon after the shooting they had very prudently set up a press conference — an unprecedented event for its time — with the three policemen involved. Their version of events — that they had wanted to capture Toplis alive, that he had shot first, and that it was his life or theirs — brought forth boundless praise for the police action in most national and local newspapers published the following day, the Tuesday of the inquest.

And just to make sure that everyone would know exactly where officialdom stood, the chief magistrate, Hamlet Riley, opened the normal, everyday proceedings of the local police court, just three hours short of the inquest, with this speech: 'I should like, on behalf of the Bench, to congratulate the Chief Constable, the Deputy Chief Constable, Inspector Ritchie, Sergeant Bertram, P.C. Fulton and Mr Norman Parry upon the skill, smartness and courage displayed in their recent capture, and to express our thankfulness that they all

181

escaped injury.' 'Capture' was hardly an appropriate choice of word to describe Toplis's fate. But then, so that no one could possibly gain the impression that his words might be misinterpreted as an attempt to influence a jury, Mr Riley added with the air of a man who wanted to explain why he had been so stinting in his praise, 'I will not say more at the present time as the inquest is pending.'

The police also had some prudent advice for the chief constable's son. Rumours were already rife in Cumberland that it was he who had shot the outlaw. Accordingly, the following morning, young de Courcy Parry walked down the town and slipped his automatic pistol into the waters of the River Eamont. It was his last memento of the trenches. Five other guns which he had brought home from the war had already been consigned to the depths of Ullswater by his father, in the same way that the whole affair was consigned to the depths of Parry's own memory. Even when he wrote his autobiography, after he had become famous for hunting foxes, not men, as the celebrated Dalesman correspondent for *Horse and Hound*, he omitted the part he had played in the Toplis story.

When the inquest opened in Penrith on the afternoon of Tuesday, 8 June, there was, as at the Shipton inquest of Spicer, a military man in the chair — Colonel F. W. Halton, coroner for East Cumberland. And although the full extent of Toplis's record and reputation had been kept secret, it was still sufficiently notorious, and the manner of his death sufficiently sensational, to pack Penrith with pressmen.

From the surrounding countryside the public flocked into Penrith and small boys played truant to attend. At the last minute the hearing was switched from the police court to the town hall to accommodate more clamouring to get inside. When Toplis's widowed, crippled mother, Elizabeth, arrived by train from Alfreton shortly before the inquest opened at 1 p.m., she had to be pushed in her wheel-chair by her daughter Winifred and an unknown male friend through hundreds of people jamming the pavements outside the town hall.

182

Mother and daughter, showing more concern in Percy's death than they ever had in his life, were photographed by thirty-six cameramen whose number included, for the first time in the history of the North of England courts, cinema newsreel operators. Although much larger than the police court, the council debating chamber inside the town hall was so crowded with officials, police and press that only a handful of the waiting crowd was able to gain entry and see widow Toplis being carried out half-way through the proceedings after she had fainted twice.

As a local newspaper reported, a 'Penrith solicitor, appeared for the police, in view of certain possibilities.' Just what these 'possibilities' were, or who was going to pursue them, was not made clear. It would perhaps be uncharitable to assume that a relative of the lawyer on the inquest jury was a further precaution against these 'possibilities'. Certainly it was an irregularity that a lawyer for the Toplis family might have seized upon. But the family had no legal representation at Penrith, just as Toplis had had no legal representation back at Shipton when the other inquest declared him to be a murderer. As it happened, legal representation on the police side was to prove an unnecessary public expense. Colonel Halton did a fine job without payment.

The coroner was surprised at the start, but quickly recovered, when Superintendent Cox, who had travelled from Andover to give evidence about the Spicer murder, did not give a confidently expected reply to the first question.

Halton asked, 'Was it proved that the man Spicer was shot with a revolver?'

Cox replied, 'Not absolutely.' And then, when he heard the court gasp, hastily added, 'But a bullet found corresponded with that of a Webley 6. We had sworn evidence at the inquest that Toplis had a Webley 6 in his possession and that he said he was going to use it to get a car.'

The police lawyer produced the revolver found on Toplis at his death. 'Is this a Webley 6?'

'Yes, sir,' said Cox.

183

Cox then went on quickly to say that the witness Fallows was present in court and could identify the revolver as the one which Toplis had in his possession in the car when going to Swansea.

Halton stepped in to say that they were not at that time further concerned with the details of the Andover murder, leaving the impression that he might return to the matter later, which he did not. The coroner had rightly reasoned that one Webley 6 looked very much like another, and that it would not help the general image should the anxious-to-please Private Fallows attempt to say positively that this was the Swansea gun. He had already gone far enough in allowing one witness to testify to what a subsequent witness would testify if called. Mr Halton therefore turned to the question of the more local Cumberland armoury. Superintendent Oldcorn told him that he had issued the revolvers and ammunition to Inspector Ritchie and Sergeant Bertram.

'Revolvers are not the ordinary weapons of policemen in England?' queried the coroner.

'No, sir.'

'And this was out of the ordinary?'

'Yes.'

'Why?'

'Knowing the dangerous character of the man, whom the suspected man was supposed to be, and also knowing that he had threatened to shoot P.C. Fulton that afternoon I considered, from a common sense point of view that these officers, who were charged with the duty of attempting to secure the arrest of the man, should be in a position to protect themselves.'

'Just further to enlarge your grounds, did you know that the man was believed to be armed?'

'Yes.'

'Have you read in the newspapers that a man believed to be Toplis had shot a gamekeeper and policeman in Banffshire?'

'Yes.'

'You knew he was a fugitive from justice?'

184

'Yes. I afterwards received the approval of the chief constable in the action I had taken.'

At this point the faithful Oldcorn is beginning to stretch credulity. He had earlier said in evidence that when he first heard Toplis was on his way he had telephoned the chief constable at home and that he had been given 'certain instructions'. Now Oldcorn was telling the court that these instructions had not included the issue of firearms, and that his chief was ignorant of the issue of guns until after the event.

Yet, without a murmur of doubt being expressed, his story was accepted, and quite uninvited, Oldcorn went on to tell the court, 'The guns were not of government issue, but I believe they were of an approved pattern.'

By now Oldcorn was floundering in his attempt to keep the chief constable out of it. In an effort to extricate himself, he continued, 'The guns were in the chief constable's possession.'

At this moment it would seem essential for Oldcorn to be asked why it was that he had so stealthily relieved his own chief of his private armoury. But, head down, Halton ignored the voluntary indiscretions. Now, just as he had urged and prodded Oldcorn to 'enlarge his grounds' for issuing weapons, so the coroner encouraged Ritchie by leading questions to declare that although there was nothing about them that could have indicated to Toplis that they were police officers, he, Ritchie, had shouted a warning before shooting at Toplis after the police had 'sprung out right over him' from their hiding place. Halton did not dwell on the points that Ritchie's exclamation, uttered when he had 'got well out into the road', had simply been, 'Stop, pull up'; and that at no stage had they indicated they were policemen.

The rest of the evidence consisted of a reiteration of the press conference account, namely, that the police had not wanted to shoot the outlaw, but that he had shot first; which is surprising enough in view of the fact that their method of disguise and concealment demonstrated clearly the extent to which the police were relying on the element of surprise.

The coroner pressed on speedily to his address to the jury, and once he had dealt with the question of identity he made the following observations:

There comes a more difficult question as to why he was killed by those police officers. The killing of a human being in England has always been treated as presumably unlawful, and amounting to wilful murder, but this presumption can be removed in certain cases. We can best get at an accurate verdict if we ask ourselves certain questions.

Where the arrest is resisted by such force as to make killing necessary in self-defence, then it becomes justifiable homicide. It has for a great many years been the recognized law of the land that where an officer of justice is resisted in the legal execution of his duty he may repel force by force, and if in so doing, without disproportionate violence, he kills the party resisting, then it is justifiable homicide. But if an officer kills after resistance has ceased, or where there is no reasonable cause for the violence, the killing will be manslaughter at the least. Also in order to justify an officer or private person in killing it is necessary that at the time they were entitled to the protection of the law.

To apply that to this case, all officers who do the killing must be officers of justice or persons in aid of them; they must be in the legal execution of their duty. That I think is apparent here. They were police officers who by their superintendent were ordered to arrest this man. In this case there was no disproportionate violence. They knew that the man was armed with a revolver. The man fired two shots at the police before they fired at him; that is the evidence of both Inspector Ritchie and Sergeant Bertram. At the moment he dropped, the man had his revolver aimed and covering the inspector.

As regards what was in the officers' minds, they knew he was Toplis, because Fulton had told them what had been said and that he was convinced of it. He had also said two hours previously that he would not be taken. The

186

deceased man had his revolver out from a few yards after he began to run. It might be said the police officers should have refrained from returning the man's fire, got under cover, and watched for a convenient opportunity to arrest the man.

If such a proceeding was insisted upon, no man at any time would submit to arrest when called upon, and the course of justice would be impossible.

Coroner Halton then laid down the line:

To my mind this case comes exactly within the definition of a case of justifiable homicide, and the police officers in what they did had both right and law on their side. They had no warrant in their possession certainly, but there was good ground for believing this man Toplis was wanted on a charge of murder, and the absence of a warrant made no difference whatsoever.

Coroner Halton had been landed with some tricky problems, but in the main he handled them well. When he referred to 'persons in aid of the police' in his summing up, he was justifying the presence of the chief constable's son. But he erred when he said Toplis was wanted on a charge of murder. Toplis had been officially and irregularly declared to be a murderer without the opportunity of defending himself.

As an ex-army colonel, Halton had necessarily been acquainted with some of the background. He was ready for his peroration.

The purpose of these Courts — and we must not overlook it — is as much to protect individual subjects as it is to bring the right people to trial, and it is up to us, to you and to me, to see that justice is done in all these cases. It is for you to say whether these officers were, or were not, justified in the action they took.

To my mind that is the only verdict it is possible for you to return. If not, then the other verdict is the one of wilful

187

murder against the police officers who tried to effect this capture.

Faced with that sort of ultimatum, it took the jury foreman, Ian Sim, just three minutes to return to say that the police were not guilty of murder. He put it this way: 'The jury find that the deceased, Toplis, was justifiably killed by a revolver bullet by the police officers in the execution of their duty.' Which particular police officer, he did not say. (Sixty years later, de Courcy Parry Jnr still maintains that he was certainly not the killer, although he acknowledges that some people continue to point the finger of suspicion in his direction. He also states that he does not know who shot Toplis.)

Sim, however, did not just leave matters at that. He fulsomely added: 'The jury also wish me to say that they believe the police acted not only with discretion and care, but that their conduct is worthy of praise; and the jury would like to congratulate all the officers concerned upon the intelligence and promptitude of their actions, especially in the case of Constable Fulton, Inspector Ritchie and Sergeant Bertram.'

The coroner joined in: 'I would like to associate myself with what the foreman has said regarding the conduct of the police. Their whole conduct seemed to have been well carried out. They showed considerable pluck, and there was no cowardice in any one of these police officers.'

The chief constable responded: 'I thank you all for your words of praise for the police. I am sure they will be highly appreciated.'

So far as the several misgivings expressed by the *Manchester Guardian* were concerned, the inquest had failed to do its duty. Most of the questions of conscience that the newspaper had raised remained unanswered, both then and in the future.

It was 2.25 p.m., and about five hundred of the crowd who had been unable to gain admission had stayed waiting outside. When reporters rushed out with news of the verdict, the crowd cheered loudly. The all-in-black Widow Toplis heard them cheering as she was smuggled out at the back of the town hall by her daughter, wheeled across a lawn into Portland Place, and into the police station, where she again fainted on seeing her son's body where it had been left lying on a large table in the weights and measures room.

The police had already allowed newspaper photographs of the sight which overcame her: a death-mask face with wide-open mouth showing two missing teeth in the lower jaw.

In rigor mortis, Toplis's tongue had stubbornly persisted in protruding through that gap, almost as if in a last act of defiance. But even involuntary insolence was not permitted; a police doctor had cut off the outlaw's tongue.

Doubtless, this seemingly grotesque intrusion was carried out to make the corpse look slightly less horrific. But with the removal of his tongue, of course, went the last risk that the monstrous mutineer might reveal all — even in death.

17

Toplis now became the property of Fleet Street. The *News of the World* and the *People* ran features. Although ignorant of the real Toplis story, they gave extensive coverage to that part of his background of which they were aware. But even their stories paled beside the inventiveness of a 'special investigator' for the *World's Pictorial News*, a Hulton paper of the day.

Toplis had been an anarchist, the ring-leader of a Free Love Club in the East End of London. The paper knew of six girls he had seduced, 'some from the higher middle classes and some who were lowly born'. Gallantly, the *World's Pictorial News* withheld their names. But alongside their other main feature, 'My Life as Vampire Queen' by Theda Bara, they regaled their readers with the full story of 'the daring adventures of Percy Toplis with a beautiful young motorist'. In the one article it skilfully enshrined every iniquity known to 1920s journalism.

How Toplis Eloped with Pretty Motorist
The daring adventures of Percy Toplis with a beautiful young motorist, whom he persuaded to elope with him — an exploit which had a dramatic ending — is here described

190

by a *World's Pictorial News* special investigator. It is one of the outstanding incidents in his amazing career.

Fake Telegram That Nearly Ended His Career

Among the women who fell victim to the fascination of Toplis was a young, beautiful, and well-to-do lady. She met the arch-deceiver quite accidentally, and was at once impressed by his manner and the plausible story he told with a ready tongue and unblushing assurance.

The woman's motor car broke down on the outskirts of Putney Common. She knew little about the mechanism of the car and was almost in despair when a stranger who was passing jumped off his bicycle and proffered his help. He was successful, and the grateful woman asked the man for his name. He was ready enough with a reply.

'I am a Captain in the army,' he said, 'and at home on leave. My name is Williams. I am not at present in uniform as I have special permission to wear civilian attire. It is much more convenient and prevents one being pestered by having to return salutes. That is one of the nuisances of being an officer, don't you know?'

Thankful for the help she had received, and pleased by the man's apparent modesty, Miss H— invited the bogus captain to call on her — an invitation that was immediately accepted.

Miss H— lived in a large house in the near vicinity, and there the adventurer made his way on the following day. He had effected some changes in his appearance, however. He was now in the uniform of a captain, and wore across his left breast the ribbons of decorations he had never won. He affected a detached and inconsequential air, spoke with a 'Varsity drawl', and still more deeply impressed his hostess.

Had she but known, the very bicycle from which he descended to render first aid to Miss H—'s motor car was stolen. It was traced afterwards to a second-hand dealer who gave a description of the man from whom he had bought it. He was Toplis.

The tales Miss H—'s guest told of his prowess on the field

191

were such as would have put the Baron Munchausen — the world's champion liar — to the blush. Yet he was clever enough to appear to make light of his achievements.

'It was nothing — only duty, you know,' he would say with a wave of his arm.

He spoke of his wealthy friends, and told an extraordinary story of his relations with his 'people'.

'My father was a soldier — an officer, killed in a little skirmish on the frontier,' he would say. 'Received a posthumous Victoria Cross. Sad for the dear old mater and for my sister, who married quite beneath the family traditions — business man with money, don't you know?'

Miss H— introduced her hero to a great many of her friends. She was proud of him, and, indeed, as they walked along Bond Street people would turn round to look at them. Miss H— declared that the notice they attracted became positively embarrassing.

I daresay that you will already have gathered that Toplis — like all criminals of his type — was extremely vain. It was one of his ambitions to 'cut a dash' and to appear as a 'squire of dames'. He never tired of boasting of his power over women. He professed to hold them in contempt, while all the time he was doing everything in his power to fascinate them, and to bring about their ruin.

At one time, indeed, he was a prominent member of a secret and infamous organization, which met in the East End of London, and which called itself a club. The declared objects of the group were to destroy the very foundations of ordered life and government, and to set loose the wildest and most violent of human passions.

One of the avowed objects of this gang of miscreants was the destruction of the marriage laws. They openly avowed the profession of Free Love. They even set about the degradation of women and initiated unspeakable orgies, at most of which Toplis was present, and was one of the leading spirits.

The club, happily, did not have a long existence. It was discovered by a lynx-eyed detective, who was trying to find the whereabouts of a missing girl. She was actually traced to a house which was used by this vicious brotherhood. The girl was over the age which entitles her to the protection of the law, and — evidently under the influence of Toplis and his friends — she refused to forsake the evil course on which she had entered. But the police officer saw to it that the scandalous combination of rascals was broken up for ever.

It was perhaps as well that no prosecution followed. Many names of people who had fallen victims to the intrigues of the degenerate must have been dragged into the light, and the divorce courts would have had an even larger list than ever.

I have before me as I write a report supplied by the man who was directly responsible for the raid that followed the discovery of the existence of this place of infamy.

It was the avowed intention of the desperadoes to make the world unfit to live in. Laws were to be defiled and society outraged.

Perhaps the worst feature of the whole business was the fact that women were to be decoyed away and subjected to all manner of indignities. They were to receive treatment worse than could have been conceived by even the most pessimistic of mortals. They were to be positive slaves — and worse. Strangely enough, Toplis was then passing under his own name. He is known by that name in certain quarters of the East End to this day.

I have broken away from the main narrative with the object of throwing the lurid light of fact upon the character and disposition of this terrible personality. Some people still regard him as a hero. He was in reality no more a hero than Charles Peace or Jackson the convict in Strangeways Jail, who murdered a warder, scaled the prison walls in broad daylight and remained at large till he was captured near the prison.

Like Toplis, this man lived by theft during the time he was at large, haunted public houses, where he treated everyone who would accept his hospitality and talked loudly about the exploits of the murderer, discussing the

193

probability of his recapture. But I must return to the association of Toplis and Miss H—. As I have pointed out, the woman spent a good deal of time in the company of the gallant 'Captain Williams'. In accordance with his usual practice Toplis made love to the lady. He suggested that they should go on a motor trip to the coast, stay there over the weekend, and afterwards get married by special licence. It was all very rapid, of course, but this 'Captain' had plenty of excuses to make, and was secretly delighted when he discovered the impression he had made.

Nothing was said concerning the arrangement to the girl's friends. That was a stipulation the masquerading Captain made. Miss H— gave out that she was going on a visit to some acquaintances and she joined Toplis at Richmond, where he had a car he had procured by using a bogus cheque. He also had some money he had procured in the same fashion. First they discussed the destination to which they should drive. Toplis must certainly have been pleased when his companion suggested a spot that was quiet and secluded. The girl was happy and trustful. The Don Juan had won her regard and had probably made use of that hypnotic power of which he boasted.

One wonders what the unhappy girl would have thought had she even guessed that the man who was riding at her side on that glorious Thursday afternoon was a thorough-paced scoundrel, an ex-convict who had done two years' hard labour for a savage and unspeakably wicked assault upon an inoffensive young man and who was even at that moment a deserter from the Army. No glimmer of the terrible truth passed into her mind as, radiant, beautiful, full of hope for the future, and of trust in the man by her side, she rode along the country roads.

It was at the suggestion of Toplis that the car was driven to Seaford and Toplis, posing as Captain Williams, drew up outside a hotel. He waved a hand to the chauffeur and told him to put the car up at some garage in the neighbour-hood. They did not stay at the hotel. Toplis took rooms at a boarding-house. The next day he broke the news to his

194

companion that he had dropped a wallet which contained not only his money but some cheque forms of a well-known military bank.

Toplis received what must have been to him something of a shock. Miss H— had very little money with her. The resourceful scoundrel, however, was not long before he thought he could see a way out of the dilemma. She must send a wire explaining that she needed money. 'Don't tell them that you are with me. They need not know that 'til after the marriage ceremony,' said Toplis. Toplis's heart must have been in his mouth when the reply came. His spirits must have sunk to zero when he glanced at the contents. Instead of the well-known pink slip indicating that money had been sent there was the buff of an ordinary message.

'Read it,' said Miss H—. 'My brother is coming here by the earliest possible train.' I expect at that moment there was no more uncomfortable man in existence than Toplis. The last person he wished to meet was an officer and a gentleman — especially when he happened to be the brother of a woman he had deceived.

What followed indicates the absolutely guileless nature of the girl. Toplis suggested that she should remove some of her jewellery, leaving it in his care. Miss H— fell into the trap. She took off a heavy bracelet, three rings — one of which was set with a glorious diamond — and a wristlet watch. Toplis gathered all the jewellery into his pockets, gave the girl a kiss and left her. Nor did she hear of him again 'til she saw his photograph and read of his exploits in the newspapers.

*

This article ended with the note 'More revelations of Toplis's secret life next week'. And, as a matter of fact, the week after that as well. Toplis had knocked even Theda Bara off the front page.

The memory of Toplis held by his niece, Mrs Phyllis

195

Kerry, who continues to live at Blackwell, is in sharp contrast to the sensational accounts of the *World's Pictorial News*. She remembers him as a loving uncle who constantly bestowed generous gifts upon members of his family, especially at Christmas.

18

The Toplis women wept their way home on the train to Alfreton on the night of the inquest, leaving a police force whose conduct up until then had been highly questionable, to dispose of the body in circumstances that were outrageously bizarre.

The police had got the verdict they so desperately wanted from the inquest coroner and jury. Now all cooperation with the Press ceased immediately. The goodwill of the visiting hordes was no longer necessary.

When police had searched Toplis's clothing as his body lay on the table in the weights and measures room, awaiting inspection by the inquest jury, they found a gold-rimmed monocle, of course, a first-class rail ticket, a photograph of, and a letter from, 'Dorothy', a pawn ticket for a wristlet watch, half a crown and a gold ring set with three diamonds. What he had separately bequeathed to the authorities was a seemingly consuming desire to emulate his deeds of deceit and disguise. And, on the Wednesday when they buried him, they demonstrated that they had well learned the lessons he had taught.

The last official melodrama started at 8 a.m. when an unidentified police officer arrived at the wrought-iron gates of Penrith's beautiful hillside cemetery overlooking the town, Ullswater Lake and the Lakeland hills and mountains beyond. To a large cluster of photographers gathered outside the locked gates, he announced that the funeral had been put back from 9 a.m. to 1 p.m. The explanation was that the coffin was not quite finished.

Tired pressmen, who had been on duty until midnight and then up half the night drinking, were only too ready to accept the word of the law and went back into town for breakfast. When, later, they found that they had been duped, their wrath was directed against the police, but the real instigators of the trick were the Home Office in collusion with the War Office, and the police a willing party. The chief constable had stated quite categorically the previous night that the funeral would be at 9 a.m., but in the interval orders had been received that if the funeral was to go on at that time, it must be in secret. And so the police, having successfully lured the press away from the scene with false information, stuck to the original plan. At 8.15 Mr Harry Bartley, a close friend and associate of the local police, and a fellow member of the Rifle Club, along with Oldcorn and Bertram, drove his mineral-water lorry into the yard at the rear of the police station.

Toplis's body, in its workhouse coffin of plain wood, with an inscription plate carrying the words, 'The spirit shall return unto God, who gave it' and 'Bless the Lord, O my Soul', was furtively, quickly loaded on to the lorry and covered with old rugs and rags. Whatever else Toplis might have appreciated about the crazy circumstances of his last journey, he would not have liked the reading on the coffin nameplate, 'Francis Percy Toplis, aged 23, 1920.' Toplis had hated his first name and had never used it.

Bartley drove his odd hearse along Meeting House Lane, up Fell Lane and along the Beacon Road, a route different from that usually taken to the cemetery. For most of the way he drove slowly, out of a mixture of some respect for his cargo under the rags and a fear of the possibility that if he speeded up the coffin might bounce off as the lorry had no sides to it.

198

But at one point he was forced to speed up when the alternative became getting to the cemetery without a body or being followed by an unwanted cortège. From his high cabin, with its oval-shaped side and rear windows, he had been anxiously glancing around to see if he was being followed. Suddenly, as he neared his destination, he spotted what he thought was a press car and upped his speed to the maximum 45 m.p.h.

As the coffin bounced up and down on the back of his vehicle, Bartley prayed that the rugs and rags would not slip off, revealing that this particular delivery run was quite unconnected with lemonade. But his fears had been groundless, for when he finally, breathlessly, rattled through the cemetery gates, the car behind him swept on past. Waiting to receive the lorry and its load was Deputy Chief Constable Barron, Inspector Ritchie, Relieving Officer Johnstone, the cemetery curator, Brunskill, and the undertaker, John Ireland. They hastily rather than reverently pulled the coffin off the lorry into the small chapel just inside the cemetery gates. Just as quickly they bolted the doors from the inside and briskly hoisted the coffin on to their shoulders up the aisle to a table before the chancel.

Bartley then drove off again to his lemonade deliveries, and the curator locked the gates behind him. Before taking up a strategic position behind shrubs, with three of the undertakers' assistants on the look-out for gate-crashers, Brunskill knocked on the cemetery lodge door to tell the Reverend Robert Law that his presence was awaited. Inside the chapel, Barron, Ritchie and Ireland impatiently occupied the front pew. Mufti was again worn by the two officers, upon whom it had been impressed that speed and secrecy were the essence, and now the tall, distinguished, grey-haired vicar was threatening the success of the operation with his tardiness. The official view had been that the parson's presence was only necessary at the graveside, but the Reverend Law had insisted on conducting a full Church of England service, his argument being, quite properly, that the deceased had not been convicted of a capital crime — a fact which authority had been inclined to conveniently overlook until now, and one which they did not want to have interrupting the proceedings.

The officers stirred uneasily and thought that the vicar was doing the occasion slightly more than the religious justice it merited when he intoned that it was not for anyone gathered within these walls to judge the wrongdoing of others. The Reverend Law did not intend to spare them. 'Circumstances have been such that this man was violently removed from this life before he could be judged on earth,' he said. 'Let his only judgement, therefore, be made in Heaven.' In the absence of music the vicar thought that the 'mourners' should follow his lead in singing the first verse only of a hymn which he presumed was known to them all. A very reluctant and markedly off-key Barron and Ritchie joined in the words, 'There is a happy land, far, far away ...'

At last it was over, and the two officers could stop glancing back at the church door and listening for the knocking that would tell them they had been detected and their little ploy uncovered. The coffin was carried two hundred yards to a grave listed as No. 7135 in the cemetery register, under a yew tree at one of the highest points in the graveyard, and when Barron and Ritchie helped to lower the coffin, they did not know that the undertaker, Ireland, had sympathetically and secretly reunited the gold-rimmed monocle with its owner. It had been placed by his side before the coffin lid was nailed down.

In the register, opposite the entry 'P. Toplis', curator Brunskill penned: 'Shot dead by police at Plumpton.' Triumphantly the police placed their prepared notice on the gates: 'Francis Percy Toplis was interred at 9.00 a.m. this morning.'

The Penrith Board of Guardians, the local public assistance board of its time, met to hear the relieving officer, Johnstone, report that the cost of the pauper's grave had been £5 9s. 6d., although they could set against that the value of Toplis's clothing and other property which now legally belonged to the board. The arrangement in fact showed a small profit.

When it was suggested that the Toplis gun should be sent to Penrith museum, Johnstone pointed out that the police wanted the gun to hang on their headquarters office wall as a memento. It was agreed to be a 'jolly good idea'.

The gun, like the original photographic print of Toplis lying dead in Penrith Police Station, only disappeared from view in 1977. In the whole of Cumbria, authority is without knowledge of what happened to them.

19

Back in the real world questions about the Penrith shoot-out were beginning to be asked with a little more penetration than the coroner had shown. The *Manchester Guardian* said the day after the inquest that the killing 'was not by any means, the best end to a bad business'. In an editorial that was more slightly hinting than hard-hitting, the newspaper continued, 'There are several minor but interesting loose ends to the story as it stands at present, and had the case of Toplis gone before a jury some of them might have been cleared up.' Letters registering disapproval of the shooting started to reach newspapers and Members of Parliament.

The London correspondent of the *Yorkshire Post* wrote:

The fatal use of firearms by the Penrith Police against the suspected Percy Toplis seems to have taken some of our sentimental politicians by surprise.

The matter is to be raised in the Commons, some members holding that the right of the police to fire on suspects should be clearly defined and restricted as much as possible.

The authorities have no quarrel with this claim; indeed

it is their own. The question of arming the police has been under consideration for some time. However, the final decision was that in view of the recent increase in crimes of the type of which Toplis was accused, and the knowledge that these criminals would not hesitate to shoot at police attempting their arrest, revolvers should be issued to police, the question of their use in exceptional cases being left to the discretion of senior officers.

The chief constable was, therefore, acting on the Home Office instructions when he used his discretion in starting armed on the hunt for a man known to be desperate enough to shoot at sight officers attempting his arrest, The view in official quarters in London is that the discretion exercised must be upheld by the authorities in spite of what may be urged to the contrary. The 'matter' was never raised in the House of Commons.

In an attempt to stem the criticism, the *Penrith Observer* fairly lashed out. Under a headline 'Facts and Gossip' it thundered:

There are sentimental, and perhaps soft-headed people who deplore the fact that Toplis was shot dead instead of merely being 'winged' ... Toplis went bad as a lad, gradually but rapidly passed from bad to worse, and the world is well rid of a scoundrel of the most dangerous type.

It was not enough to lay the spectre of these events. By now the 9,000-strong population of the old market town were buzzing with rumours that not by any standards had the whole truth been revealed about Toplis or his violent end. So the *Penrith Observer* tried again. It suggested that the police had undisclosed information, and that their erratic behaviour had been the result of outside pressure. The article continued:

The Chief Constable, the Deputy Chief Constable, and certain other responsible officers, did all they could to

203

place at the disposal of the Press whatever information it was advisable to make public.

Much in their possession, of course, was of a highly confidential character, and it would have been greatly against the public interest to have allowed it to be published. The police headquarters were besieged by reporters and photographers from all parts of the country; altogether there must have been over seventy in the town, but they were met by unfailing courtesy and received the greatest help.

Some of this proved to be undeserved, as irresponsible and unscrupulous men, when their turn had been served, published matter that ought to have been regarded as confidential. Others, in their feverish search for stories, broke well-known rules, and might easily have caused great trouble to those concerned.

At the top of the list of secrets could only have been the fact that Toplis, who had been a deserter on and off for over three years, was not merely a monocled outlaw. He had also been one of the main motivators of a dangerous mutiny about which no news must ever be allowed to leak out.

Certainly the Cumbrian establishment were sensitive to the feeling that all had not been correct in the Toplis killing. Only a fortnight after the inquest, the Standing Joint Committees of Cumberland and Westmoreland had the resignation of Chief Constable de Courcy Parry in their hands. The tough ex-boxer, ex-Derby County FC centre-half, was leaving after eighteen years in charge. Superintendent Barron, his deputy, presented his departing chief with a silver rose-bowl and a signed photograph of his senior officers. He made a point of the fact in his speech that the chief's health 'had broken down under great strain'.

Superintendent Barron then saw his own name safely on to the short-list, and waited confidently for the Committee to appoint him Chief Constable. To his consternation, and the fury of his friends on the local paper, he was passed over. A new chief was brought in from Scotland. The *Penrith Observer* regretted: 'It is a curious fact that an officer, who for months together, during the last two years, has carried out all the duties of the Chief Constable was not thought deserving of the permanent position.'

But the police committee was most anxious not to give any immediate endorsement to an affair which considered opinion was coming to see, as the *Manchester Guardian* had put it, as 'a bad business'. The frantic consultations with London, the army and the Home Office on the night of the ambush were now becoming known. If the chief constable and his deputy had indeed submitted to pressures from Whitehall which, at best, laid no emphasis on taking Toplis alive, then it was better for a new figure to take over the force with his reputation, and particularly his independence, untarnished.

In due course, Norman de Courcy Parry, formerly Chief Constable of Cumberland and Westmoreland, was given a Whitehall appointment as Inspector of Constabulary. It was promotion; apparently his health had recovered. He had already been made a Commander of the British Empire. Inspector Ritchie, Sergeant Bertram and Constable Fulton did not have to wait so long for their reward. The Penrith Town Council felt able to make a payment of £10 each to Ritchie and Bertram, and £15 to Fulton.

Fulton, who retired from the police force with the rank of sergeant, died in 1977, leaving de Courcy Parry as the sole survivor of the 1920 Sunday night ambush.

*

Another man followed with special interest the death of Toplis and the rise of the legend in the newspapers.

At Vevey in Switzerland, Brigadier-General Andrew Thomson, RE retd, perused the *Continental Daily Mail* anxiously for any hint of the dark secret of the mutiny that he and the army had so successfuly conspired to conceal. There was not a whisper about his encounter with Toplis, the man who had consummated his disgrace. The secret was to survive a further fifty-two years after Thomson's death in February 1926.

205

Thomson left behind £12,004, and an obituary in *The Times* which dismissed his war service in one sentence: 'In the Great War he was mentioned in despatches and was specially employed in Holland in 1918.' He never set foot in England again but he does have one last obscure memorial, a faded photograph in the Sandhurst Collection.

And now that the full story is known the thoughts of Lieutenant James Davies, too, go back to those days of 1917. After that he lost a leg at the battle of Amiens in August 1918. Demobilized, he returned to England and went back on the stage. During the Second World War, he became Britain's only one-legged infantryman, serving with the Indian Army and having two bullets shot through his tin leg in a skirmish on the North-West Frontier. Now over 80, he lives in retirement in the Cotswolds.

And, still defying the British Army, Percy Toplis has his own place of honour — gazing arrogantly down from a photograph on the shelves of the Imperial War Museum, dressed in the uniform of a lieutenant. Old soldiers and their exploits never die, nor do they entirely fade away.

206